FOOTPRINTS
In my Rearview Mirror

*An Autobiography and
Christian Testimony*

By

George Oiye

PRESS

Table of Contents

Prologue

Hello! Please come on in and leave your footprints on my rearview mirror. As we grow through life, many people cross our paths and leave their footprints or tracks behind and we leave a few as well. If you would like to take a look at eighty years of the indelible ones that have contributed to shaping my history, just grab a cup of coffee or something, curl up and enjoy surfing through my biography that looks like a rolling surf where the sea meets the sand.

Preface

Footprints In My Rearview Mirror is an anthology of anecdotes that represent the qualities and quantities of many footprints that have imprinted the life of a second generation Japanese American boy, who was born in a log cabin, on the continental divide of the Rocky Mountains east of Butte and west of Helena, Montana. Here it gets minus sixty to seventy degrees below zero in February and March and the snow completely covers the cabins nestled in the pine trees at the Josephine Mines. Rimini, Montana was the closest small mining town that took six to eight hours to reach on home made snowshoes. This little town of forty or fifty people, living in log cabins and corrugated tin shacks spread out along a little creek, served as a resource for supplies, services and a social contact for a first generation Japanese immigrant named Thomas Jengoro Oiye or Tom Oiye, as he became known.

Tom and Taka Oiye

O*iye is a very uncommon Japanese name. There are many spellings for the name depending on the prefecture where it originated. Some times it is spelled Ohye, or Oye, or Oi, or Oiye. Normally, Japanese pronounce every vowel phonetically, with the exception of this name where it is pronounced Oi, like boy. My wife and I choose to pronounce the "ye" as well, thus Oi-ye, sounds like Boy-yea. For laughs, we tell people that we are Japanese-French.*

My father came to America from Fukuoka, Japan at the age of about seventeen and worked on fruit and vegetable farms in and around Seattle, Washington. He also worked in a lumber camp around Olympia, Washington, but his small five-foot stature limited what he was allowed to do. He then got a job on an Alaskan whaling boat that harpooned whales, using a cannon to launch the harpoon. This was a very risky and strenuous job that he liked that taught him a lot about the sea, whales and Eskimos. His long-handled mustache made him look very mature and cocky for his age.

In 1917, Tom like many other single Japanese men went back to Japan to get married according to the oriental customs of the time. In Japan the parents of the bride and groom prearranged marriages. Tom's parents were farmers and he had finished middle school as a math teacher before coming to America. Adorned in his striped woolen suit complete with vest and huge railroad watch including a gold chain watch fob, he was introduced to Taka Kimura, the fifth and youngest daughter of a sake merchant who also lived in a seaport town of Fukuoka Ken on the Island of Kyushu, Japan.

Taka had a very keen and acute tasting ability and could tell what field or country that rice came from once she had tasted it. Rice is the basic ingredient of sake and can control the taste of the wine. Her father used her as his quality control person. This unique skill remained with her throughout her lifetime.

After their very formal Shinto style wedding ceremony they stayed in Japan for two months and bought steerage class tickets, at the bottom of a Japanese freighter bound for Seattle Washington. The two or three week Pacific Ocean trip to Seattle was everything but pacific. Newly wed strangers going to a strange foreign land to establish a home and family was a terrifying experience for Taka. How young couples could and did make those marriages last is beyond my comprehension. *As a follower of Jesus Christ, I am convinced that the Grace of God reigned in their lives.*

Fortunately, Tom and Taka were able to get jobs as house-boy and house girl with a wealthy, highly educated Swedish lady in Seattle. This was a bonanza for them because she taught them everything that they needed to know to survive in America. My mom learned to read, write and speak perfect English, she learned how to sew and became an expert seamstress making suits and dresses of all kinds. Cooking and baking Swedish pastries was a specialty that forever became mom's trademark in rural Montana. She learned the value of cleanliness and doing a quality job. With these skills Taka bought a fifteen-cent per night flophouse and cleaned it up and changed the sheets daily. Her hotel business was doing quite well at twenty-five cents per night.

My father was also very literate in English and well known for his farming skills. He and his partner had learned that Japan was using blood meal as a high nitrogen yielding fertilizer and were importing it from Seattle. Since the slaughterhouses were glad to have someone to clean out the blood from the trenches the two men went from place to place gathering up the animal blood and drying it and making blood meal. This product was shipped to Japan for a good profit.

Like most starry-eyed young people blinded by gold in their eyes, my parents were eager to sell their businesses to a fast-talking gold miner that stayed at my mom's hotel. Little did they know that they had bought a share in a defunct placer mine in Montana?

It was near the end of the big gold rush to Montana, in August of 1921 when Tom and Taka Oiye, with their two daughters Peggy 3-1/2 yrs old and Anita 1-1/2 yrs old set out from their home in Seattle, Washington to make a fortune in Montana. They arrived at Basin Creek, Montana in late August of 1921 by train and were taken to the mine by horse and buggy.

Mom said that she had fifty cents worth of cash left over, after buying clothes, supplies and food that was to sustain them for a long hard winter.

Tom learned the art of panning gold and running the placer along with trying to cut enough wood to keep the nearly starving, young family warm and alive when the bitter sub-zero weather arrived. On February 19, 1922 a son was born and named George the beginning of a long and complex life filled with many footprints that have blazed the off-road trails for this book.

Footprints

*P*eople leave one or two footprints that run through other lives and sometimes they gradually increase to make a path, which becomes a trail, that turns into a rutted road, to highways, to a freeway, and on and on into one's fading memories from gold mines to war, to aerospace and large lasers but never quit. Some of them are but little puffs in the dust or snow while others are huge craters and ruts in the mud that leave big scars or become great indelible lessons about life as one passes through the world toward eternity. Just getting old is a sterile way of life but growing old gracefully is a God-given gift.

People and events mentioned in this book are real and are recorded as accurately as possible, so as not to misrepresent anyone or anything, many unclear parts that do not have distinct tread marks have been left out.

CHAPTER 1

The Beginning

Porphyry Dyke Mine
[1921-1924]

The Word

In the beginning was the Word, and the Word was with God, and the Word was God. He was with God in the beginning. Through Him all things were made; without him nothing was made. In him was life, and the life was the light of men ... The Word became flesh and made his dwelling among us ... full of grace and truth...." Ref. John 1:1&14 (NIV) (New International Standard Version, Zondervan 1985)

This story starts here and ends here for it is the foundation and thread that runs throughout and holds it together with authority. As you will see, so far it has taken God eighty years to shape this unique life into what he began and has put my name on... *"I have called you by name; you are Mine! "When you pass through the waters, I will be with you; and through the rivers, they will not overflow you.*

When you walk through the fire, you will not be scorched. Nor will the flame burn you. For I am the Lord your God...your Savior." [Is 43:1-3] (New American Standard, Holman 1980)

Note: The source of all other scripture references will be identified as used, throughout.

Mike

Are you Mike? These were the first spoken words that I remember saying when a man named Mike brought my parents supplies on his wagon during the good weather.

It was always the highlight and excitement of the future to listen for the distant rattling of Mike's buckboard wagon and snorting, steaming horses as they picked their way up the steep rutted trail to our cabin on a regular basis. After the exchange of greetings came the treat of an apple, an orange, a Hershey Bar, Wrigley chewing gum, Sunkist raisins in small boxes, or nuts for George. Just the anticipation of the smell of the gum wrapper or Hershey Bar was enough to keep me standing by the fence and shivering for hours with wet pants and wet shoes waiting for Mike, a man without a face; but with a huge voice and heart behind that silhouette made the first imprints on my life.

Gold

The Anglo-Saxon word gold is aurum in Latin and designated Au. The word has a certain aura to it that draws one to it and often defies good sense. Many gold-miners have struck it rich but they are far outnumbered by those who have chased rainbows.

I have learned that gold does not always come in pure or

free form and only very few fortunate miners have gotten rich picking up nuggets. Even free gold is usually hard to extract from the quartz that it is most commonly associated with. However, at the Josephine Mine, west of Rimini, gold existed in the porphyry dyke rock formation in several forms, some nuggets called free-gold, some in powder form called gold-dust and some chemically bound up in the rocks. A porphyry dyke is an igneous intrusive geological domelike formation, mostly of feldspar, which contains loosely, bound sapphire crystals, nuggets of tin [cassiterite], gold, silver and other minerals.

Much like granite, porphyry that is exposed to the elements decomposes in the severe freezing cycles in the winter thus freeing up any pure minerals making up its structure. The loose decomposed earth can then be easily collected by hand panning or by use of a sluice box called a placer. In large operations, gold dredges that float on water; semi-automatically load the gravel into the placers by buckets attached to conveyer belts and is processed aboard the floating placer.

Another form of gold mining is to use chemicals to leach the gold from the low-grade type of hard rock ore after it has been crushed.

Tom's job was to pan the riffles in the placers to collect the free gold and to check the tailings for any free gold that might have gotten overlooked. Since the tin and sapphires were not very valuable at that time in history, it was all discarded with the tailings. In modern times the sapphires have become valuable gems; the free-tin ore has also been recovered and sold for a profit using modern equipment.

Ironically, some friends from the laser industry have re-opened that mine to claim the low-grade sapphires. They precisely process the low-grade sapphires into expensive gemstones by heat-treating to control the color.

First Lesson to Learn

When you dig in the garden and find a horse shoe, you must spit on it and throw it over your left shoulder and it will bring you luck, were some of the first words that my father taught me.

Over the years, I have recklessly tossed the horseshoe into various windows, flowerpots, and even into people throughout my life; so the luck hasn't always been good luck; but horseshoes and the smell of horse manure leave indelible tracks in the process of my history. How many times in our lives have we been stepped on by a horse or mule or nipped in the back pocket by one, as the cinch got tightened?

Montana Sunset

What a treat to be carried on my fathers' shoulders while my two sibling sisters ran ahead as my parents took us up the trail to a high point to wait for the dazzling sight of a Montana sunset of bright reds, golden oranges fading into deep purples as the sun was being swallowed up into pillows of clouds. As we all huddled together on a big rock or grassy spot to savor the moment, our additional reward was to indulge in a Hershey bar or a stick of Wrigley's chewing gum. Just to sit there and to lick and smell the wrappers in the crisp clear mountain air and to enjoy the experience was a lasting moment accented by the chirping of squirrels, singing of birds and a cool breeze. Running down the trail to get home before dark was always a challenge for the girls to keep from skinning their knees and a rough ride for me while hanging on to my fathers' ears, hat, forehead or anything convenient to stay on board.

Fall

While I straddled a log on a sawhorse, my father used a bucksaw to make the log into winter firewood.

The birds singing in the meadow and the bees swarming as they buzzed around an old log were signs of late summer and fall that went along with the crisp cool air and trickle of water in the nearby creek that would soon ice over and become silent. It would soon start snowing and an English couple; Dave and Anna Thomas would pack up and head for Rimini for the winter. Mr. Breen, the owner and superintendent of the mine, gave Tom his instructions for the winter and also packed up and left in a snowstorm. Even Mike stopped coming there with supplies.

With the gentle breeze and smell of musk in the air, one does not have to be an adult to sense that something is going on in the fall with the coyotes howling, dogs barking, bull elk bugling and locking horns, and buck deer snorting and fighting for supremacy. To watch them doing something and not understanding what all the ruckus was all about doesn't escape my very young memory.

Winter

Sometimes when the snow quit falling and the sun came out; Tom would take a large stick and find grouse, called fool hens. He would hypnotize them by slowly winding the stick around and around until he got close enough to hit the bird and kill it before it could fly away. Needless to say, we all looked forward to those days of feasting which were followed by long days of being snowed in and supplies running low. Tom would then head out for Rimini on his homemade snowshoes and be gone for days while Taka and the three nearly starving kids stayed in the log cabin waiting and anxiously listening for any signs that papa had returned. By God's grace he always came home and we all survived the bitter cold winter months from October through April.

Spring and Summer

The snow began to melt in late spring and it was a surprise and learning experience to see the fields of flowers popping out of the snow in all colors, shapes and sizes in great profusion. What an excitement to bring a handful home to mamma, but it made her cry. And then, the mushrooms popped out and we ate well along with edible fern sprouts, trout, and grouse. A very short summer limited the garden to fast growing vegetables, which my mother and father competed with the deer, birds, skunks, rabbits, squirrels and bears to get a handful of pre-chewed on carrots, potatoes and cabbages. Papa always knew what animal left its teeth marks and showed me how to tell some of them.

Deceived

In the late fall of 1924, it became apparent that the gold mine was defunct and the Oiye's had been deceived. They would now have to pack up and leave their log cabin and their rainbow behind and head for Helena, Montana to look for other work. Their first stop on the long wagon ride was at their friends the Sparrings' house in Helena. Ice and snow made walking very slippery and Taka fell and cut her eyebrow badly. Blood on new white snow covers a large area and is bright red, which gives a nearly three-year-old boy a trembling fright and the girls cried. The cold snow served as a coagulant and Mrs. Sparring put a big white gauze bandage on mama's eye and it healed.

I have often pondered and speculated what pathway our

lives could have and would have been if my parents had kept their businesses?

The Chopping Block

While at the Sparring's house, I met two of their sub-teen aged boys and the older one wanted to show off how good he was with an axe; so he told his younger brother to put his thumb on the chopping block and he chopped it off in one blow. More blood, more panic, more screaming and yelling and much scurrying around took place. Dave and Mrs. Thomas came to the rescue and only those footprints of that incident remain. *The ending of the Oiye's saga of not getting rich looking for a pot of gold in Montana was only the beginning of their learning that there is really no free gold in ones life; even though God is good, life is tough.*

Helena, Montana

Helena , Montana, the gold rich capitol of Montana was a very large city compared to Rimini. It had about 20,000 people and was the railroad center for the Northern Pacific railroad and the agricultural and mining center of Lewis and Clark County. The Thomas', the Sparrings', and the Oiyes' started a new life here. For me it was a frightening place to be with its fast moving and smoking cars, engines that belched fire smoke and steam and made lots of big noises. The rattling and swaying street-cars, huge buildings made from stone and red bricks, strange noises, lots of smoke, funny looking clothes, funny looking people, strange languages, cowboys and Indians roaming the streets, loud talking and fist fighting men, and people who chased Japanese and Chinese kids.

Helena was a place of many firsts for me as the big earthquake of 1925 came rumbling to town knocking all of the chimneys off the houses, opening up cracks in the streets, skewing the sidewalks, knocking brick walls and buildings down, derailing trains. Cats and dogs howled and ran from place to place some even had fits and frothed at the mouth. It was here that the Big Top Barnum and Bailey Circus came to town and my parents took, the now four kids, brother Ben was born in February of 1925, to be awed with the wild animals, cotton candy, Ferris wheels, side shows and magic. Two hung-up dogs going down the street back to back, with their tongues hanging out is a puzzling scene for a bug eyed 3-year old boy to see.

Mister Ogata

Renzo Ogata, who lived in a Japanese Camp near the railroad round house, befriended the Oiye's and found Tom a job at the round house shoveling ashes under the big coal burning steam engines called malleys. This job was very hot and the sulfurous smoke was acrid and choking. Sometimes the ashes would fall down faster than they could be shoveled and his clothing would catch on fire. One time my father took me to see what he was doing and the heat singed my eyebrows and sunburned my face. The big turntables made a frightening grinding sound as they rotated the big engines. Even though I was hot, I was shaking with fright as the fire, smoke, and steam belched out of many places from the engines as they moved from place to place and I squeezed my dad's hand with my first white knuckles. Hell must be a terrible place.

Like my father and mother, Renzo and Mrs. Ogata came to America with the dream of getting rich and returning to Japan to retire because the 1924 Asian Exclusion Act excluded them from getting citizenship and owning land in America. Renzo was a very bright man and extremely enterprising. He was also a leader among his fellow men and started a camp for them along the railroad tracks, near the round house, where he piped in raw steam from the round house to provide hot water for their Japanese style bath and for heating the tar paper shacks that they lived in. Mr. Ogata spoke very good English so he interpreted for his Japanese-speaking friends. One of his enterprises was to raise vegetables for food and he sold the excess to the grocery stores in Helena. What impressed me most about Mr. Ogata was his five-foot stalky stature, his perpetual captivating big-toothed grin, and bursts of barefoot energy all held together with his bib overalls that seemed to hop and scurry about at a chipmunk's pace.

CHAPTER 2

The Character and People of Trident, Montana

[1926-1942]

Trident, Montana

In late 1925, Tom Oiye heard about a Cement Factory in Trident, Montana that was hiring foreigners to work in the factory and rental of the company houses was cheap, so he went there and applied for a job to get away from the hot round house. He got a job working for the Three Forks Portland Cement Company and moved his family of six to Trident in 1926.

In Latin mythology a trident served as a three-pronged fishing spear that symbolized a sea god, such as Poseidon. The three tines of the fork represented the three rivers that joined at Trident, Montana to form the headwaters of the Missouri River. Fittingly the Three Forks Portland Cement Company's logo was "Red Devil Cement" that depicted a red devil with a long spearheaded tail and he carried a three-pronged pitchfork, a trident. He had long pointed ears, a Van

35

Dyke beard and his whole body and head were clothed in a long red union suit. About 1937 the Red Devil Brand was replaced with a generic term Ideal Cement Co. The Portland in the company name designates the type of cement for making concrete and has nothing to do with the city in Oregon.

The wealthy Charles Boetcher family of Denver, Colorado owned the company and became very famous. In 1928, a big black cloud hung over the Boetcher family and the town of Trident, when their only son was kidnapped and murdered. Not only were the residence of Trident feeling the effects of the Great Depression; but, along with the whole nation they spent anxious moments and hours glued to their Philco radios and reading the newspapers that came by train, to learn about this tragic event.

Railroad Tracks

Railroad tracks, seems to be such an innocuous term today and only applies to a small part of our transportation system. But, in its early years, the railroad tracks were not only the power of empire builders and the lifeblood of history; they were also the dividing line in society.

People's state in life was always associated with which side of the railroad tracks that you lived or came from. Even in a little rural town of Trident, Montana, if one lived in WOP Town, it was a degrading and an undesirable identity. *Only, by God's grace did the Oiye's live with the "White Folks", so to speak.*

For the kids the railroad tracks was a playground. They were the doors and windows to the outside world. We learned the dimensional reference measurements in numbers of steps and the size of a mile between signposts and the roadbed was a great source of ammo for sling-shots. The cross ties made good firewood; just practicing balancing on one rail was fun and healthy. Smashing things by letting the train run over them changed pennies and dimes into treasures. Who needed a clock when the trains ran on time?

(Of note is the fact that in the culture of the day, a man's state in life was measured by the size and brand of his very accurate "Railroad Watch" timepiece and gold watch-fob-chain.)

During the depression years, hobo's came from every-where on the rails looking for work. Some of the ones who stopped over and lived in the "Hobo Jungles" brought with them sociology, geography and philosophy as they spun stories about life with the wide-eyed kids. Hobo's also provided the mischievous kids with moving targets for their sling shots as they went whizzing by on top of the boxcars, inside of the cars and on the bars under the cars called "riding the rails." I wonder what our lives would have been like without the trains and hobos?

The Northern Pacific railroad tracks divided the town into two long narrow strips of land bound by the Missouri River and the rock quarry that ran east and west at this geographical location.

The Right Side of the Tracks

The residential side of the town was about 100 yards wide and 400 yards long and was shaded by big cotton wood trees whose roots caused the cement sidewalks to heave unevenly and were very bumpy that made fun roller-skating. Trident was a small company town of maybe twenty or thirty lath and plaster, houses with a basement that had a heavy lift up door that gave many smashed fingers and battered hands. These basements were dark and dank and the creaky steps were always a challenge. The field mice and pack rats competed for residence in the basement.

They provided kids and cats with great sport and sometimes piggy bank pennies for catching them. A pack rat is a very strong animal with razor sharp teeth that can gnaw its way through a 2x4 board in minutes. They are characterized by carrying or packing things that intrigue them from one place to another until they find something that they like better and drop off what they have in their mouth and trade it for the newfound treasure, thus the name "pack rat." One got all kinds of neighbor's things that sometimes branded you as a thief.

The houses had from four to six rooms and the rent ranged from $12.00 to $17.50 per month depending on the size and location. The plant superintendent and the chief chemist lived next door to one another on the east end of town and had the expensive houses rent free, as part of their job compensation. Ironically, although recorded history states that the houses were only available for non-aliens, my alien parents had one of the houses and did not live in WOP Town. This was never a contested issue that I know of. Maybe it was because they had papers.

A dirt road alley running parallel to the river and railroad tracks divided the houses into two rows the full length of the town.

All of the houses had little back yards with various kinds of clothes lines where the clothes freeze dried in the sub zero winter weather and looked like cardboard men and women dancing on the clothes lines, that often sagged to the ground from the frozen ice. The wind had lots of fun chasing the frozen clothes down the alley when the wooden clothespins popped off. Meanwhile the fat alley cats licked the cream off of the tops of the frozen milk bottles that sat about an inch under the waxed paper cap above the milk bottle.

Garden plots faced the alley where rusty, smelly, fifty–five gallon oil drums were used to collect trash and garbage that was hauled off by a horse and wagon dray to WOP Town where an open pit dump that was constantly kept burning. It was a smelly, smoky, dangerous place for a kid to play and off-limits, but some naughty ones fell in and got burned anyway. On a hot summer day, flies and maggots lived in the barrels that reeked from rotting garbage. They were often tipped over by skunks and dogs spreading the garbage down the alley. Winter was less smelly but had its problems with wet garbage freezing inside the barrels or the barrels sticking to the frozen ground, so garbage pick-up day was always a noisy day as Ole' George Haggard beat on the barrels to break them away from the ground or to loosen the contents of the barrels.

Recycling

Everything was recycled, bed sheets and clothing were home made from the printed flour sack material, but not before the men women and the kids all learned to knead bread from the flour and to sew, mend and iron the flour sacks. Competing with the mice and rats for the flour gave rise to creative flour bins. Twenty-five pound empty lard cans with lids were the most common flour bins. Cats and mousetraps kept the rodents under some control. Sugar and rice came in one hundred pound sacks as well and had to be stored in dry mouse-proof containers. Walk-in pantries provided ample space for storage of the large containers and cooking equipment. The smaller five-pound and ten pound, baled lard cans also provided handy storage and utility containers called canisters. Galvanized dairy milk cans made fine containers and seats as well. Orange crates, apple boxes, and all fruit boxes made good temporary furniture and utility boxes or kindling wood. The fruit wrappers, except peach wrappers that contained peach fuzz, were saved and hung up in out-houses on a large pin or nail.

String balls, bent nails, rusty bolts and nuts, baby food bottles, coffee cans, tin foil balls, bags and old car parts were all common items in mom's bag of tricks or in ones basement or garage.

WOP Town

The east side of the railroad tracks was the industrial side of Trident that covered a strip of land about 200 yards wide and about a half mile long, with a railroad-siding and a switching yard, the cement plant was adjacent to a rock quarry.

Situated across the railroad tracks from the store, there was a two-story office building, which had a chem. Lab, and several upstairs rooms for single men to rent. A horse barn and company garden plots covered about three acres of ground west of the office building and further west was a 200 foot diameter gravel pit that was a great place to catch pollywogs and frogs.

To the east of the office was an on-fire dump and a corrugated tin shantytown called "WOP Town" for Italian immigrants and alien foreigners. WOP was an acronym, created by the National Immigration Service that meant "With Out Papers." Since the predominant group of aliens was Italians, the town was identified with Italians or WOPS.

The town of Trident was supplied with water from a well near the river that was pumped up to a water tank on top of the quarry hill east of the cement plant and had a pressure head of 150 to 200 feet or 75 to 100 pounds per square inch [psi]

The rock quarry had one huge steam shovel and one smaller diesel driven shovel that loaded up five-ton dump trucks with rocks that had been blasted down and jack hammered into small manageable chunks. It was hauled to progressive rock crushers where it was crushed into small pieces. There were catwalks between the crushers and flying ropes were used to control some of the processes.

Speed Lewis

Speed Lewis, one of the workers got tangled up with a rope and it pulled him up to the ceiling and wrapped him around a rotating shaft. An emergency shut down was made, but too late to save his life. Workers had to be very alert to work under the primitive and dangerous conditions that existed throughout the plant.

Sometimes explosions occurred in the quarry that killed the men in the tunnels or near the blast site and showered the town site with flying stones. Often times in cold weather the rock driller's glove would freeze and stick to the drill bit and break his arm. There were many places where the workers were exposed to machinery that was red hot and got severely burned. In general the plant was not a safe place to work.

Shooting the Rings

Periodically the smoke stacks for the kilns would get plugged up with a ring of slag and clinkers. These rings were shot at from the firebox with an 8 or 10-gauge shotgun. The process was called "Shooting The Rings," which made a loud noise and showered hot dust, sparks and slag downwind all over the countryside. This was quite a sight to witness when it was done at night. Of course, all of the workers wanted to be the gunner and everyone came out to watch the fireworks. After crushing, the rock was burned, or dried at a high temperature in horizontal forced-air coal-burning kilns. These rotating kilns were elevated at a small horizontal angle so that when the rock reached the bottom of the kiln it was completely dried and was ready to be progressively ball-milled and furnace-fired at [2200 Deg. F.]

Gypsum and iron was added and milled until a specified fine gray powder was produced. Throughout the process chemical analysis and tensile strength tests were performed by Mr. Burkett to maintain a specified quality of product.

Silos

Storage tanks or silos were used to store the cement prior to bagging and shipping. A transport screw line ran under the silos to collect the cement that was coming, simultaneously, from all of the bins or silos in small-regulated streams. The screw line transferred the liquid like powder to an elevator that dumped the cement into a bin that fed the Bates Machines. My father, Ed Olson, ad Speed Lewis ran the Bates Machines.

Mud swallows built their nests under the eaves of the silos and the kids made great sport of shooting the mud houses down with their ever-trusty slingshots, sometimes called "nigger flippers." *I'm uncertain where that currently unacceptable expression came from.*

Bates Machines and Tunnels

A Bates machine was a semi-automatic bagging machine that filled and weighed the cement bag to ninety-four pounds, or one cubic foot of raw cement.

The bag was automatically released to a conveyor belt that went to a chute in a boxcar, where truckers were waiting to take turns to stack six or seven sacks of cement on their hand-truck that were wheeled to the end of the empty boxcar and emptied. In a busy season, when the storage bins get low, the cement may come almost direct from the ball mills and be very hot. When this happens the entire equipment line gets hot as well and becomes quite hazardous and risky to the workers.

In about 1932, nine silos thirty feet in diameter and about one hundred feet high were built to increase the storage capacity of the plant. All nine silos were built simultaneously and used an ingenious screw jacking system that allowed the forms to be raised on top of the concrete as it cured; but it had to be jacked up at a constant rate, twenty four hours a day until the job was finished and the forms removed.

Buried in Cement

One summer I had the job of running the tunnel under the silos and had to keep the screw line flowing smoothly; everything was working just fine when one of the silos had an internal slide causing the feed gate to overload the screw line. Before I could shut it off, I was up to my neck in cement. The end result was that the screw line overloaded the elevator and shut it down. When the elevator jammed, it caused the Bates machine to shut down and my father knew that something was wrong in the tunnel so he and the entire crew came to my rescue and dug me out just before I suffocated. To be buried in cement that weighs ninety-four lbs. per cubic ft. put a lot of pressure on my body and totally immobilized me. How I survived is just one of God's miracles that I can't explain.

Cement Bags

Originally cement bags were heavy canvas bags that were wired shut on one end and had a self-closing filling hole on the other end. These bags were returnable and required a great deal of maintenance work to keep them in service. When the bags had been wet they were returned with cement set up and clinging to the surfaces, both inside and outside. These bags had to be cleaned in an eight-foot diameter rotating drum made from heavy-gauge, perforated, steel sheet with an array of heavy bicycle type chain flails, called beaters. Clean bags, without holes were tied with a copper wire by a tying machine that took a double looped wire and twisted it around the neck of the bag. Clean bags with holes or tears were sent to a sack shed where they were patched by sewing or hot gluing a patch on the inside of the bag.

One of my jobs was doing all of the bag maintenance operations. This was a big job and took a lot of logistics to keep the Bates Machines supplied with bags. During the winter months my father patched sacks and earned money to pay the rent. Eventually, strong, disposable paper bags were developed and replaced the canvas bags.

Social Security

Working in the cement factory were very special days for me that allowed me to mature rapidly and to earn three dollars and twenty cents a day, just like my dad.

In 1937, when Roosevelt started Social Security, I got my Social Security card and number, at age fifteen.

Long before the days of Ralph Nader and the EPA (Environment Protection Agency,) the cement dust was so thick that it coated everything and denuded the hills of grass and vegetation for miles around. Pure white washings seldom existed and one's skin was always irritated from the raw lime in the cement dust. The prevailing wind was usually from west to east so that the school yard and beyond was usually quite crusty. It was common practice for the workers to coat their hands and faces with Wesson oil or lard to keep their skin from drying out. Hair was always very dry and brittle. *If you didn't have hangnails to chew on and bleeding cuticles you were a sissy.*

Ole' George

George Haggard was the company drayman and we all learned a lot of choice things to shout when something went wrong, which was very often. Ole' George had a long and bushy, well stained, handlebar mustache and an old felt hat that looked as if he was born with it. He and Maude, his wife, were like a comic strip and the neighborhood kids would tune into their favorite soap opera to get in on the latest rift. One cliché that characterized Maude, was that she always ended up every argument with, "Geeeoooorge don't argue with me because you know I'm right!" No matter how the kids treated Maude and George, they were always good to the them and made us cookies, paid us to bring slop for the chickens and George was always giving the kids horse and wagon rides or sleigh rides or letting us play in the barn and let us feed the chickens or gather eggs.

Pool Hall/Barbershop/Bowling Alley

A pool hall/barber shop/bowling alley, an icehouse and a double row of garages made up the border on the west side of town. During the prohibition years a pool hall and bowling alley were incorporated into the barbershop as a cover up for an open bar and gambling house. It is rumored that the old speakeasy way of life existed for a number of years at the barbershop.

Silent Film Movie Theatre

A silent film movie theatre that still stands today was a high-ceilinged, long narrow building without windows, about 25 feet wide with a floor which sloped to the front. It had a stage, an orchestra pit and a foot pumped organ. A narrator sat on a stool to the left of the screen and provided an exciting description of the story and the voices to the movie characters. He or she also provided the supporting sound effects that the organist couldn't produce. Some of the regular narrators were professionals and had a lot of class; but the bad ones were quite awful. High up in the back of the theatre was the projection room that leaked light and the carbon-arc-lamps gave off hot, bright bluish white lights to project the picture from a 35mm celluloid filmstrip to the screen. The flickering projection made the movie hard on the eyes but it added to the mystic of the movie as the projection beams shone through the blue overcast haze of cigarette and cigar smoke that filled the theatre. Before fireproof film was invented, whenever the projector jammed, the film caught on fire and the projectionist had to put out the fire to keep the theatre from burning down. Wisely, the town architect had put the towns fire wagon at the end of the theatre building facing the alley and large barn doors were on the entry for quick exit. Charlie Chaplain, The Keystone Cops and the Dead End Kids were the favorite kids movies with popcorn, peanuts, and Cracker Jacks all for less than fifteen cents. Sometimes we could sneak in for free and sit in the back row loges. At other times kids weren't allowed in so we took turns looking through our favorite cracks and peepholes to watch Clark Gable kissing Scarlet O'Hara, which was a no-no.

Mrs. Hove

Next door to the theatre was a two-storied hotel run by the Karl Hoves', mostly for single men. The building was about thirty feet wide and sixty feet long. The second floor had about sixteen rooms and two baths. The lobby, dining room and kitchen and family quarters were on the first floor. It was also used for large meetings, weddings, and etc. The kitchen was a very busy hungry smelling place and the coal burning stoves, boiler and steam radiators took a great deal of coal to keep the place warm and with meals and bath water.

A Wool Blanket

I was seven years old when Mrs. Hove asked me if I would like to have a job carrying coal from the basement upstairs to the kitchen? Because I slept outside on our makeshift front porch, I needed an extra blanket for my bed for the fifty below zero winter weather; I jumped at the chance to get my first job. She asked me how I would like to be paid and my quick response was, "I'd like to be paid every two weeks, just like the men do." It took eight months, at a rate of fifteen cents a week to be able buy a wool blanket from the "Monkey" Wards catalogue for my bed.

It was all that I could do to drag and pull the big large hotel sized coalscuttle up two flights of steps and into the kitchen coal bin. At first Mr. and Mrs. Hove helped me and later built some steps so that I could do it myself. By the time I had earned my blanket, I was a strong eight-year-old kid able to make it up the stairs without stopping and do it in one-fourth the original time. This commitment taught me a very valuable lesson in my life.

When Mrs. Hove sold the hotel to the Eldor [Ed] Olson's, Mrs. Birdie Olson and their four girls, Enid, Edna [Gillespie], Georgia [Wellhouser] and Lena continued to add tracks to my life's path and to help me earn money to buy fishing poles, reels, line, hooks, a 22 rifle and shells. Although the hotel is now gone, the valuable lessons remain.

The Trident Store and Post Office

On the east side of the street from the hotel, was a two-storied, combined mercantile store and post office run by Henry and Hattie Carver. The store stocked everything from jawbreakers to furniture and was not only the place for high school kids to congregate and to catch the school bus to Three Forks, but it also served as a hub for the entire towns activities. There was a street that ran from the riverbank between the hotel and the store all the way crossed the railroad tracks to the office building. This road divided the town from east to west, while the alley divided it from north to south.

Mister NA Smith or Smitty

A railroad depot, adjacent to the railroad tracks and across the street from the theatre, sat on a small hill about six or seven feet above the road. This hill was a favorite place for the kids to play, especially in the winter when it snowed.

Happy go lucky, Smitty was the depot agent and telegrapher. He was very fast at sending Morse code with a dit-dah key and became a very valuable person, especially during the war.

N.A. whistled a lot and was always looking for ways to help the kids have fun. His two daughters, Charlotte and Norma were much older and experienced than most of our contemporaries. They were our neighbors, so us siblings inherited a lot of their 1920's flapper kind of stuff to play with like high heeled shoes, ostrich feathers, big straw hats, lip stick, nail files, nail buffers, fancy dresses, button shoes, curling irons, phonograph records and, etc, etc. Both boys and girls had fun acting older. Sometimes the Smith's gave us an exciting ride in their big Buick. In 1931 Beulah Smith died of bone cancer so Smitty moved to Whitehall.

Chet and Bertha Young

Chester Young became Smith's replacement and lived next door to our family for about six years. Chet and

Bertha were wonderful neighbors and friends and remained loyal until they both died in about 1990. They moved from Trident to go to Western Montana near Kalispell. His replacement was Lloyd Hayes from Whitehall.

Mister Hayes

The Hayes moved next door to our family in Trident in 1937. Mr. Hayes was a man with a perpetual grin. He, like N.A. Smith was a happy-go-lucky man with only good things to say about everything and he sincerely enjoyed kids. He was a collector of old shot guns and did some gunsmithing and restoring old shotguns as a hobby.

Mister Gardner

At the far eastern end of town, between the railroad tracks and the riverbank was a two-room schoolhouse and teacherage with a basement. The heating system for the two buildings was down in the basement where the janitor, Hugh Gardner, a fifty-year-old Scotsman had to stoke the furnace early in the morning before school started. One cold winter day a big mountain lion trapped Mr. Gardner in the basement and he couldn't come out until school started and one of the teachers ran for help. A second grader doesn't forget how hair raising that can be. The Ledingham family was quite shaken up because Hugh was Mrs. Ledingham's brother. Jack Ledingham was my contemporary and feared for his uncle; but Buster the oldest boy, thought that the whole scene was quite funny and laughed.

The Schoolhouse

This schoolhouse had a "little room for grades one through four" and a "big room for grades five through eight." It was situated half way between the railroad tracks and the riverbank at the very east end of town.

The playground consisted of a tennis court, ring bars, merry-go-round, swings, small track field, trick bars, and teeter-totters. Heavy willows, nettles, chokecherry bushes, thistles, wild rose bushes and a steep bank along the river were off limits as were the railroad tracks; but we played there anyway.

The play yard was crusted over with hardened cement dust which was very alkaline and dried out ones skin and hair. Surrounding the schoolhouse and by the tennis court was a small grass lawn that was cool in the summer. Another no-no was an old abandoned concrete cesspool that bordered the schoolyard to the east where the river and the railroad tracks came together. The top had caved in, in a few places and hobos from an adjacent hobo jungle used it for shelter. Some time the big bad boys would sneak a peak into the dirty place and get covered with the dried up sewer sludge.

The Island

About a quarter of a mile west of town was a branch channel in the river that formed an island on the opposite bank from the icehouse and Kirkhams' house. A rock dam about 10 feet wide was built across the channel about 100 yards west of the garages to close it off. A two-foot diameter, galvanized pipe was buried under the dam to provide a small flow of water to the slough during high water. The dam provided an access to the island and formed a slough for making ice in the winter. Beaver and muskrats lived in the slough when it had water in it as well. The island became a favorite place for the kids to play and for the Mikelberry's to graze their cows. It had thick willow groves along the banks that provided sticks for the gardens and for making slingshots, bow and arrows, and whistles.

Cottonwood trees grew in abundance on the island and provided firewood and nesting places for crows, magpies and other birds. It was also a favorite place for the boys to make clubhouses in the willow groves. Some of the big boys would wait for the crows and magpies to nest in the trees and blow their nests and baby birds up with blasting caps that they stole from the rock quarry dynamite shed.

Driftwood

The Missouri river was about 75 yards wide, in the summer and about 150 yards wide, in the winter and sometimes overflowed its banks during the ice jambs in the winter or high spring run off. Huge piles of driftwood collected on the island and provided firewood for ice-skating parties, swimming parties and for smoking. Some of the towns men would trap skunks, coyotes, badgers, beavers, muskrats, weasels and rabbits that lived on the island and slough to supplement their incomes. Stray cats and dogs found good hunting and shelter here.

Piles of driftwood on the island that were replenished every spring during the high waters were very functional. They provided firewood for the cookouts, campfires, skating fires, and decorations for the homes. Unique to the cottonwood root driftwood is that it has tiny longitudinal holes in it and is quite porous. It can be puffed on when lit on one end and smoked. Parents allowed the kids to smoke driftwood, as it had no nicotine; but the smoke was full of tar and stained ones teeth and fingers. If it were too dry it would catch on fire and would bite ones tongue. Girls particularly liked smoking driftwood at skating and swimming parties because its original shapes were distinctive and fashionable.

In the winter time the river usually ran full and the slough filled up with water to about six feet deep. When the cold weather set in and the temperature got down to thirty or forty degrees below zero or even colder the slough froze over to three or four feet deep making ice for the ice house which sat on the bank about fifty feet from the Kirkham's house.

The Slough and Ice House

Putting-up ice for the summer was a whole town affair that lasted for several days in the middle of winter when the ice was cold and thick. First the barn-like icehouse had to be cleaned out of sawdust and any old ice. Then a long wooden chute about two feet wide was set-up from the slough to the icehouse. The ice pond was swept clean and a starting hole dug through the ice until water was reached. Men with large crosscut saws cut the thick ice into one and a half-foot by two-foot blocks and as thick as the ice was frozen, perhaps three to four feet deep. These large blocks were grabbed with an ice tong hooked to a rope and pulley/winch that a team of horses pulled up the ramp and into the icehouse where men with tongs grabbed the big blocks and layered them inside the icehouse. As the layers built up, new sawdust was shoveled over the ice for insulation and the ramp was raised and adjusted for the next layer. The process had to work quickly to prevent the ice pond from freezing over. As the ramp got higher and higher the process got more dangerous.

Sometimes the tow rope broke or the tongs slipped and the ice came back down the chute and the ice-cutters had to get out of the way to keep from getting hurt or thrown into the pond. Some of the less agile men like Hugh Gardner often fell into the icy water and had to be rescued and thawed out. If the ice came up the chute too fast and the men at the receiving end weren't fast enough or strong enough to grab the block, it would knock them down and sometimes cause serious injuries. When there was not enough ice to fill the icehouse, then the operation was shut down and it took several days or weeks to refreeze new ice.

The ice was then distributed throughout the town for the ice boxes, which usually held a block of ice about one cubic foot to one and a half cubic feet, that lasted about a week. As the ice supply diminished, the icehouse became a neat cool place for the kids to play in the hot weather.

The slough became a skating rink and place for Brewer Johnson to use his goat to pull kids on a sled down a track that he cut into the ice, in the winter. In the summer time, until the slough dried up it made a good fishing and swimming hole. When the slough dried up Ralph Mickelberry used it to graze his milk cows. The cockle-burrs grew profusely in the slough and it was always a challenge to get through there without getting your socks full of burrs, a bane to moms.

CMStP&PRR

The electrified Chicago Milwaukee St. Paul and Pacific Railroad ran on the far bank of the Missouri river and had to be riprapped with large boulders that provided the railroad bed and excellent places for fish and game to hide. High above the railroad tracks on top of the rocky bluffs that abounded in many large rattlesnakes and cacti and were not good places for kids to play; but the large high-tension power poles with long ceramic insulators made for good sport to vandalize and to often shoot down for rifle and sling shot practice. These were the same bluffs that Lewis and Clark first viewed the headwaters of the Missouri River.

The Milwaukee Railroad originated in Chicago and went as far west as Seattle, Washington. The Rocky Mountain Division of the railroad ran from Harlowtown, Montana to Avery, Idaho. Mr. Tom Koga ran an oriental extra gang on that division and Mr. Fiske ran a substation at Eustis. John Satake was Mr. Koga's assistant and Arthur Hamaji [Hama] was in charge of the gas-electric tamping machine. Three Forks was the dividing line between Harlowtown and Deer lodge, Montana. At Three Forks a branch line ran to Gallatin Gateway where a grand hotel was built as a connecting point with a touring bus to Yellowstone Park via the Gallatin River. Near Belgrade, Montana another branch line went to Bozeman and followed the Bridger mountain foothills to Ringling, Montana where the railroad connected to the main line east to Two Dot and Harlowtown.

Donut Cave

Overlooking WOP town, about two hundred feet above the road, was a cave with a hole in the middle that from a distance looked like a donut.

This was another place that the Burkett and Oiye kids played. The view from there, after the rattlesnakes were cleared out of the cave, was worth the hard slippery climb.

As we grew older we would venture up to the water tank hill and shoot gophers with a 22-rifle or snare them with a fly rod, the latter being the most fun trying to pull them out of the hole in the ground or keep them from getting back in once they were pulled out. Sometimes rattle snakes four or five feet long with several gophers that it had swallowed were snared or shot in the same area. They looked funny with pea-pod lumped bodies slithering along in the dust.

Mister Ledingham

In the winter we would ski and toboggan down the same hill. Mr. Bob Ledingham made a toboggan for the kids and eight or ten of us used to come down the hill very fast. One time when we got to the steep gully, at the bottom of the hill, the toboggan broke in half and Mr. Ledingham got skewered by the broken boards and was laid up for most of the winter.

The Horseshoe Hills

About four miles west of Trident were the Horseshoe Hills where many homesteaders had ranches that went defunct when the 1925 earthquake caused the springs to dry up and the hills to become dry land. Homes with everything left in them, were abandoned and only the ankle deep dusty roads remained as evidence of a once thriving community. Not even birds or rabbits could be found. One time, Boyd Lehman, the Burkett boys, Jack Ledingham, the Ronning boys and I walked back to those houses and came back with a couple of one horse shays that we road down the hills until the wheels fell off. I found a silver dollar in the dust on the road to Recap and kept it for many years until our family pooled our money to buy a farm in Logan.

The Dry-cleaning Man

Jacking up the dry-cleaning route man's car so that the wheels spun when he tried to go to the next house was great sport to watch from a distance in the dark. When he raced the engine we would yank the jack out and the car would lunge ahead and hit the end of a rope tied to the back bumper. The poor driver hated to come to town in the evening because the kids were always laying in wait for him. The girls enjoyed this as much as the boys.

Shivaree

Shivaree is an unheard of term today for a mock celebration or hazing of a newly wed couple. To celebrate the wedding of the newly married couple, the whole town came out on the streets on a Friday or a Saturday evening and took turns running the faceless couple around town in a wheelbarrow while everyone hazed them.

Lots of beer and hard cider flowed and rising out of the dust was a lot of gaiety. The poor worn out couple would eventually get delivered to their apartment or house and get dumped on the front porch or carried off to bed. Sometimes, several events took place in close succession.

The Burkett's

Alonzo Burkett came to Trident in 1916 to become the assistant chief chemist of the Three Forks Portland Cement Company and later held the prestigious job of chief chemist after marrying Nina Armstrong , from Big Timber, Montana.

They had a family of four children and lived at the far eastern end of the town, on the riverbank, next door to the superintendent's house. The siblings were the same ages as the Oiye family kids and became our best and most loyal friends even until this day' seventy-five years later. Helen was the oldest and paired off with Peggy; Bill was second and the same age as Anita; Bob was the same as George and Norma was one year older than Ben, our youngest. These two families of kids shared every joy and heartache of going to grammar school and high school and growing up together during the great American depression years that made up the original warp and the woof of our later lives.

Alonzo and Nina are both uncommon names that are easy to remember when I associate them with all of the wonderful qualities of their individual characters and role models as American citizens that they were to us. Alonzo was a dignified, quiet gentleman with a huge smile punctuated by a Wellington pipe and characterized with his leather putties and pegged pants. Nina also had a genuine big grin with a bit of humor and a twinkle in her eye to go along with it. This was reflected in the genes of her family. Our family was of similar nature and treated each other in kind. Regardless of their status in life, the Burkett's always treated us as their equal. Mrs. Burkett, whose birthday was on the same day as my brother Ben's will always be remembered for his third one, when they met in the alley by the store and she said to Ben "where's a piece of your birthday cake for me?" He quickly responded, "Well, I don't see any of yours coming trotting down the alley." Until she went to be with the Lord she always laughed about that funny scene.

Bill Burkett

Although Bill was two years my senior, he was my best friend and confidant. I don't know if I inherently liked older friends or if it was a trend that started by being pals with him. Older boys always knew a lot more and had a lot more to teach me, usually the naughty things, they were a lot bigger and tougher and protective of me; so I didn't have to do all of my own fighting. The excitement of adventure, both make-believe and real was the highlight agreement of being with Bill.

Smoking cigarettes was the popular thing to do among the older crowd and like all Tom Sawyers and Huck Finns we wanted to smoke too; so at seven years of age the older boys gave the others and me a puff on a cigarette. Our parents got wind of this and put a stop to it; but in all fairness and in defense, the mothers made some rules about smoking. We were allowed to smoke coffee grounds, tealeaves, driftwood, Indian tobacco [a weed], and corn silk and almost anything except tobacco. The mothers even saved and dried the coffee grounds and tea leaves for us. Both boys and girls fashionably smoked all of these things including dried horse manure, either in a home made corncob pipe or rolled up in newspaper or cigarette paper when we could get it. The end results were not exactly nice to look at because it stained our teeth and fingers and the loose ersatz tobacco would fall out and burn holes in our clothes. Striking kitchen type matches with ones thumbnail often burned and blistered the thumb while the cigarette went flying through the air landing on something and leaving a scar or starting a fire. If one used the seat of his pants to strike the match, it left streaks in the denim and sometimes caught them on fire. As time passed by, the ersatz tobacco gave way to the real stuff and a five-cent bag of Bull Durham or Golden Grain brands, the cowboy's favorites, became popular. Rolling a cigarette became quite a challenge for the boys and we would spend days at the cabin learning how to roll a cigarette that the tobacco wouldn't run out the end or be too fat in the middle and fall apart from too much spit or poor quality paper. One-handed rolling of a cigarette was the epitome of smoking skills, which very few of us achieved.

One time Bill and I hooked a seven-mile ride on a freight train to Logan and back and wouldn't have gotten caught and double punished if our cigarettes hadn't come apart and burned holes in our shirts.

Real Tobacco

My father and the other working men at Trident took to smoking homemade cigarettes out of Prince Albert, Sir Walter Raleigh, or Velvet brand tobacco that came in pocket sized tins or one pound cans. He liked the moistness and smell of Velvet so bought it by the pound and I would help him roll up a few days worth of cigarettes at a time. When the fox is in charge of the hen house, like some businessmen, I would skim a bit and didn't have to collect cigarette butts to smoke. At fifteen, when I got a job working in the cement factory it became acceptable for me to smoke tobacco and chew tobacco as well. By this time cigarette-rolling machines replaced the hand rolling method, except for the cowboys and die-hard smokers who still hand-rolled with one hand.

Bill and I learned how to use a cigarette paper as TP too. What you do is fold the paper in half, tear out and save a half-moon hole in the middle, now put your middle finger in the hole, wipe with your finger and then wipe your finger with the paper. Oh yes, I almost forgot, clean under your fingernail with the saved piece. Voila!

The first cigar that I ever smoked was at about age ten when Bill and I were over on the island making brandy out of fruit and sugar in a ceramic crock that we brought from home. Two weeks later, we sampled the brandy and got a little tipsy and glassy-eyed. Bill fell down on a dead branch and hurt his back and skinned up his side. When we finally staggered home Mr. Burkett, thought that we had been smoking tobacco so he sat us down and gave us each a cigar and said that, if we wanted to smoke, he would help us. Can you imagine what a mess two drunken boys smoking their first cigar would make? I don't think that he ever knew that he had punished us for the wrong crime. I did not smoke another cigar or get drunk again until I was in the army ten years later and not without getting sick.

Celluloid

Mister Burkett owned a fancy Buick Commander touring car with side curtains made from celluloid, which Bill and I found to be great sport burning holes in them with a cigarette until one of the windows caught on fire and burned the whole canvas touring cover off of the car. I don't remember what the results were but I'm sure it wasn't pleasant; strong discipline, common in those days seemed to have worked okay until Dr. Spock came along.

My pal Bill had a bicycle when he was about twelve

years old and faithfully took me wherever he went, what a friend. It was a mile out to the red bridge where Art Pyfer lived in a little shack on the Gallatin River bank. We used to ride out there to smoke Bull Durham cigarettes, to listen to his tall tales of life in the early days of Trident, and to drink his cider vinegar that seemed to be something, which we craved. There were many chokecherries for us to pick along the riverbanks in the late summer and early fall. This, of course, was more weight for Bill to carry on his bike that usually got the wheels out of alignment or bent the axles.

The Entrepreneurs

Bill and I were quite enterprising and started a window washing business for fifteen cents a house. Our very first job was a disaster when we put the stepladder on the plate glass window of Mrs. Carver's house and had to replace it. Our next enterprise was to baby-sit for twenty cents a night. One night we were baby sitting for the Honiker's two babies, and we had a big earth quake that rumbled and shook the house like a roller coaster. We were so frightened that we left the kids and ran out on the street to pull our hearts back into place. After it was all over we went back in the house and found it in shambles and the two kids were sound asleep. We didn't tell the Honiker's about that for many years later.

All about Pipes

In college, during that era, pipe smoking was not only popular, but it was almost essential to give a male student identity and class to go along with the log-log-duplex slide rule hanging from the belt. Pipes came in all shapes and designs from curved Wellingtons to a straight "Medico" with an air cooler and a filter that could get pretty raunchy. If the filter was not changed often, an occasional big slug of tar and junk unexpectedly came flying through into ones lungs causing a fit of gagging and discomfort. In any case it took a special ritual and personal discipline to properly break-in a new pipe and to build up a good dry cake in the bowl that smoked sweet and cool. To keep it that way was easier said than done because there was nothing worse than to smell the smoke from a sloppy pipe smoker's pipe. Sometimes while one had the appearance of deeply studying a serious math or engineering problem, just grooming the pipe and rubbing it on ones nose to polish the real fine burl was better than a cup of today's Starbuck's coffee.

Chomping at the Bit

While searching for solutions to problems of life, the bits on my many pipes got to be pretty ugly after hours of heavy chewing and literally chomping at the bit.

I think that more effort went into making sure that one's pipe was properly attended than learning anything about the subject, it's sort of like petting a dog or stroking a cat while reading. One of the real benefits was that it served as a live companion and helped to keep one warm in the attic room of the boarding house during the winter.

How to keep a pipe lit with an occasional puff became quite an art to avoid smoking mostly matches made from phosphorus and sulfur that spoiled the flavor of the smoke and was brutal on the lungs. This skill required the use of a tamper, usually made out of aluminum, to keep the tobacco packed down to the proper density for clean dry burning and coking of the bowl. Puffing on a pipe while lighting it requires one to bite on the bit, suck in through the nose and exhale through the teeth without inhaling or losing the pipe. In the real cold weather, being all bundled up with mittens and a scarf almost insured trouble.

Pipe Tobacco

Pipes have to have something to smoke in them and there were as many kinds and brands of tobacco as there were pipes. The cheaper common grocery store varieties like Prince Albert, Velvet, and Sir Walter Raleigh gave way to Heine's brand that came from Holland in a blue can with a painted windmill and had a wonderful fragrance. When I got a can or two of Heine's for Christmas or my birthday, it was like going to heaven. At times when Heine's was not available an American brand called Honey and Maple mixed with Sir Walter Raleigh was a good substitute; but plugged up the filters quickly and smoked rather wet, requiring several pipes always drying out. It is an obvious conclusion, that although I was a mechanical engineer, studying smoke stacks and furnaces at the time, I did more practical research and learned more about pipes than I did about chimneys and coal.

Pipe Smoking Benefits

During WWII it was nice to be among the crowd that had learned the benefits of pipe smoking and to have the battlefield diversion that it provided. On the battlefield it was worth the risk of keeping it lit without divulging one's position, especially when you were wet and freezing cold Although, smoking tobacco was considered an evil and contrary to pleasing God by some people, for me it was never evil and provided a crutch that I needed to help me through some tough years of growing up. Later on smoking became a very dirty and unhealthy habit for me and for those around me. I gave it up at the age of twenty-nine and have not smoked since.

What Kids do for Fun

The limits of what kids did was tempered by the Golden Rule which we learned in Sunday School and by our own ingenuity that gave us a lot of latitude to use the natural resources for our fun. So, the Burkett kids and the Oiye kids found it especially fun to drag a big bag of stuff down the railroad tracks to Hobo Canyon to have a cook out of baked potatoes, real weenies, marshmallows, dill pickles and corn on the cob. This place was beyond the school house about half a mile and was hard for us to get to because the railroad ties were too close together for one step and too wide for a giant step, so we tried to keep our balance and walk the rails. This was hard because of the food that we had to carry was hard to balance.

Walking along the side of the tracks was not easy since the gravel was sharp and cut through our thin tennis shoes and the banks sloped dangerously into the big river. We had to be very alert to watch out for rattlesnakes that were abundant in the hot summer months coiled up along the tracks ready to strike.

Baking the potatoes required digging a small pit and building a fire in it. When the fire turned to coals, we threw the potatoes on top of the coals and covered the whole thing with sand, and built another fire on top of that one. While this fire burned down to coals we cut willows sticks for roasting the weenies and marshmallows. When the potatoes were very black and soft to a jackknife they were dug out and eaten, leaving our faces as black as an alley cat adding to the fun. When those weenies popped open and got charred, there was nothing that tasted any better except maybe, the marshmallows when they caught on fire and got all gooey.

Mister Latimer (Lat)

Mister Latimer, the plant superintendent, had a real heart for the kids, so he set aside a small house back of the hotel and next to a row of apartment houses as a clubhouse for the girl and boy scouts. One cold winter night my brother Ben, about eight or nine years old and Bill Burkett were the last to leave the club house, so they decided to stoke the fire with coal and neglected to turn the damper down low. About three o'clock in the morning the fire siren went off and the whole town came out to see the clubhouse on fire. Ironically the firehouse was across the alley and since it was well below zero degrees, the pipes and fire hoses were frozen. There was a car parked next to the clubhouse that had all four tires flattened by the kids who didn't like "Tiny" the owner because he protested the use of the clubhouse. Needless to say, the house and the car burned down in all of the commotion.

At the risk of his winter job and a place to live, my father and brother Ben went over to see Mr. Latimer the first thing in the morning to confess what happened and to offer to work for the payment of the damages. Mr. Latimer said, "Tom because of your honesty and integrity, you don't owe the company anything and you can keep your job." I don't think I would have had the courage to do what my brother and father did and would be still paying for it.

Lat as he was called, was a big quiet sort of man and one winter when the town's men and boys were fishing at a small opening in the ice on the Missouri River at the gravel plant; he and his son Gordon, a teenager, joined us on the ice. It was well below zero degrees and we had a fire going with a pot of coffee to keep warm. All of a sudden we saw Gordon floating in the water and his dad, without regard for his own safety, jumped in to save him. Since the edge of the ice was thin it became a dangerous job for the men to quickly lie down on their bellies to form a human chain to rescue Lat and Gordon before they went under the ice covering the river. Only by the Grace of God did the men save those two without falling in themselves. Well, Lat and Gordon came to the fire to warm themselves for a few minutes before driving about a mile to their home. In about an hour Lat came back and thanked the men for their heroic deed.

The Feistner Family

About two and a half miles west of Trident was a dairy farm owned by Sam Feistner. Sam and his wife Anna had nine children, the youngest five years my senior and the oldest about my father's age. Except for John and Martha, who married John Stockburger, the Feistner family all lived together at the ranch. I got to know the whole family very well because my father worked in the cement pack house with John, Bill and Joe and we also cut wood for Sam Feistner for several years in exchange for our winters supply of beef and pork. My father and I learned that if you cut green cottonwood when it's frozen that it cuts and splits easily and makes the best-cured wood for next season. Old dead dry cottonwood is so tough and stringy that it is almost impossible to cut with an axe and doesn't burn well.

Hunters and Trappers

The boys all lived in small bunkhouses and chewed and smoked tobacco. Their conversations were about hunting and fishing and never about farming, except Carl, who told me all about making honey.

Otto, Joe, Walter and Leonard were the best hunters and trappers in the whole area and taught me almost everything I know about hunting birds and big game. Joe was my favorite hunter and he became a deputy game warden so I learned about the rules of hunting from him. Our family was well stocked with deer, elk, ducks, geese and pheasants when times were rough and we had to eat off of the land and rivers. Otto Feistner was a skillful trapper and had a live zoo of wild animals on the ranch; the most interesting and vicious was a badger that would charge anything that moved and could dig a hole a foot wide and two feet deep in just minutes. For Otto it was quite a job just keeping the zoo animals fed with mostly fish that were abundant in the many rivers that bordered their land. The story of John Colter escaping from the Indians and hiding in the beaver dams along the Madison River occurred upstream in that vicinity. The Lewis and Clark Expedition passed through the land and the three rivers forming the Missouri river surrounding the Feistner Ranch that is now a State Park. Can you imagine being a boy growing up in such a historical place?

Alma Feistner

Alma, the youngest daughter never married and helped her mother keep house and cook for the whole crew three times a day. She was an excellent cook and I ate a lot of huge farmer type of meals with them that consisted of lots of meat, potatoes, gravy, biscuits, milk and coffee.

Lost in a Blizzard

While elk hunting in the Squaw Creek/Swan Creek area of the Gallatin River drainage, Leonard Feistner and I got lost in a blizzard and walked about thirty miles in the rugged alpine peaks before we found our way to a Ranger station where we got a ride back to our car late at night. That was a wet cold and somewhat scary hunting trip. We were exhausted, hungry and aching and didn't see an elk, which was probably a good thing. Flashbacks of the "The Lost Battalion," story often occur when I recall this episode with awe and respect for the creator and his angels.

A Good Elk Hunt

One cold New Years Day I went up into the Bear Creek country out of Ennis, Montana with Walter Feistner and shot six elk near the top of the Madison Range of Mountains. We dressed them all out and put a stick across the ribs to allow them to cool off and went home for the night.

The next day we bought extra licenses for my brother and sister and one of his brothers. The weather went below zero overnight and the carcasses froze stiff as a board. We had the most fun that I've ever had bringing out an elk because it was all down hill and we could get inside the body cavity and go down hill like a toboggan on the hair. If the hill got too steep we would turn around and go down against the hair, which acted like a brake. When we ran into trees, the elk would bounce off and keep on going. We didn't have any horns or legs to worry about because we were meat hunting and only shot cows and calves. Life wasn't all tough, cold maybe, but worth it

Carl Johnson

Carl Johnson, Brewer's older brother worked on the Northern Pacific railroad and lived in a bunkhouse near the section house and he lived to hunt and fish. From his name, you can tell that he was a Swede and big and lanky. Carl was like the famous Bob Marshall, a man of the mountains and a hiker. He never gave any thought to stuffing a sandwich in his pocket and handful of raisins and head for the wilderness, or sometimes with a long cane pole for fishing. His rosy red cheeks and smile with a smirk characterized his countenance.

Although Carl was fifteen years my senior, he always invited me to go hunting with him. One January day, after the war, we drove to Gardner, Montana south of Livingston and went elk hunting in the Bassett Basin, bordering the Yellowstone Park. The snow was so deep that I wore my hip boots and followed Carl's six foot four inch stride in snow up to his waist. When we got on the fresh trail of an elk, my thirty-inch stride was more like running, to barely keep up with Carl, in snow up to my chest.

Twenty-five miles and eight hours later we got back to the car, without an elk and I was so exhausted that I didn't care. Carl always told his friends that I'm the only person that could keep up with him hunting and always wanted me to go with him. It takes a big ego or something to take on those big, long legged hunters, with lungs like furnace bellows that I always hunted with. But, they were also very strong and trail wise so I didn't have to do much when we got something.

Uncle Lloyd's Whoopee!

The Carver's, who ran the store and US Post Office were very fine, honest people and helped many poor struggling families through the depression years by extending them credit until the plant re-opened. Mr. Carver always had candy and gum for the kids. When Henry Carver died in 1932, Lloyd Carver, alumnus of Stanford University, gave up his law practice and came back to Trident to run the store with his mother. He was a popular, handsome, fun loving young man with a bright yellow Oldsmobile, with a rumble seat, that was always loaded down with kids and girls and it was called the "Whoopee."

Uncle Lloyd as, Merceille Neville his cousin knew him,

lived in a bachelor apartment over the store. As his eyes slowly failed, Bill Burkett and I spent a lot of time with him joking, giggling and laughing about life in general. When WWII took Bill and I away, he hired the Lower boys and Dave Miller, all from Willow Creek to be his seeing-eye companions until he passed away in 1977. In 1943, Lloyd, a fair and unbigoted person was willing to write a letter to the United States Army Air Corp on my behalf to vouch for my loyalty to my country. From the time that we came to Trident until Lloyd died, the entire Carver family, including his sister Lois Neville and cousin, Merceille Neville wove in and out of the Oiye family's lives. Merceille taught me how to play tennis and helped me to find my first four-leaf clover that I pressed in an encyclopedia. She and my second grade school teacher were my first heart throbs because they cared about me by always including me as a special friend.

The Ronnings

Across the tracks near the west end of the barn was a two-storied railroad section house built by the NP Railroad. Matt Ronning was the section foreman stationed at Trident. He and his family lived there. Bob was the oldest boy, and then there was Esther, John, and Clarence [Itta].

Clarence was my age competing physically in school athletics. Punching our biceps with our middle knuckle as hard as we could, to see who could raise the biggest welt, was a favorite school ground pastime. Pole-vaulting with an old bamboo pole, held together with black friction tape, and a ten-foot high bamboo crossbar entertained us and helped us win the district track meet at Manhattan in the spring. Even the sawdust in a shallow gravel pit felt good to land in.

Hey Itta!

Hey Itta! *"Go catch me some Lings,"* was a familiar quote. Matt Ronning like many of the section foremen came from Norway and had an appetite for fish, especially for burbots or lings as he called them. The Missouri river had an abundance of ling fish before the river was dammed up at Toston; they are a smooth skinned, boneless fish like an eel and grow from a foot long to four feet long and weigh as much as fifteen pounds. The meat is very white and sweet and good to eat, but not a sporting fish or popular among the general public. Ling fish usually feed at night along the river bottom and live in rocky places that have good hiding places. Matt hired Itta and me to catch them for him at a penny apiece, regardless of size. Since we also caught trout on our setlines we got two cents a piece for them.

When the fishing was good we made pretty good money for a couple of grammar school kids. The routine was to get worms from the garden and catch suckers after school on the island or near the hobo camp at the east end of town. We then cut bait into chunks and baited our fifty foot long lines and carefully lined the bait up in a shallow peach box so when we threw them out from shore they would go out without getting tangled. We would set about four or five of these lines along the shores before dark and pulled them up early in the morning before school.

Itta got a rowboat and we would set long lines (200 feet long) near the gravel plant and sometimes we caught a boatload of fish. The secret to this kind of fishing was to have railroad bolts or nuts as sinkers tied to the setline every twenty-five feet so that the line would lie on the bottom of the river from the setlines end to end. The maintenance on these setlines was important to keep them clean and from rusting, or rotting and untangled. During the school year we had a hard time staying on schedule.

Clarence brought out the devilish character in me and we often played pranks on his mom, such as using a sling to throw eggs at her, from a hundred yards away, while she worked in the garden, just to hear her cuss at us in Norwegian. *I often repent for doing that evil thing.*

The Big Boys

B ob Ronning was a buddy of Buster Ledingham; they were the big bad boys around town that exposed me to a number of premature things that a normal kid shouldn't know. One time they stole Mr. Ledingham's car and went to Bozeman. Driving at a high rate of speed they hit a horse drawn wagon carrying a load of pole going downhill and sheared the top off of the car. Miraculously they didn't get killed and the car was repairable. While the car was being repaired, in Manhattan, they stole it again one summer night and went speeding down the highway without a windshield or top or lights. An oncoming car didn't see them and ran head-on into them totaling both cars and sending the two men to the hospital. The two men were Matt Ronning and Bob Ledingham, their dads, who were on their way to check on the progress of the repair job. The Ledinghams later moved away to Helena and bought a new model 1936 Terraplane car.

The first and last time that I ever went 120 MPH in a car was when I went to visit Jack and Buster. Buster took us for a ride in the new car and floor-boarded the accelerator to see how fast it would go. The speedometer pegged at 120MPH on a curvy road on the way to Butte and my white knuckles and sweaty palms ended my association with the Ledinghams. Again, only by God's Grace am I still here.

One time when I went duck hunting with Buster in the wintertime, when the slush ice was flowing down the river, we shot a duck and it landed across the river at the confluence of the Madison, Jefferson and Gallatin Rivers. Buster took off his clothes and swam across the river and brought the duck back. We built a fire and cooked the duck while he warmed up. The stories written by Lewis and Clark and the iron man feats that they performed to discover the Headwaters of the Missouri river unquestionably came to life there and left a lasting footprint.

The Game Warden

Whenever the name of John Ronning comes to mind the story of how he escaped the game warden surfaces. It seems that Helen Burkett and John were close friends and my mom liked them both a lot, so when John was fishing on the island without a license the game warden took out after him and Helen ran ahead to our house and asked mom to hide John, which she willingly did. The game warden was not as street wise to the short-cuts and trails through the willow bushes to town, so he got lost and John escaped. It was one of our favorite stories for many years even though it has double moral standards. My mom never did like game wardens for some reason and I didn't either.

Big Jim Nelson

Big Jim Nelson who lived next door to the Kirkhams on the riverbank and crossed the alley from us was a big guy and was my dad's guardian angel. Sometimes it pays off to be small [five feet tall] and to have a love for people in such a way that the big guys look out for you. Everywhere that my father went and everything that he did, Big Jim was always there to protect him or help him. Jim's wife was called Nellie and his two kids were James Jr. (Judd) and

Gertrude (Gertie). The siblings were highly disciplined by their mother and were targeted for pranks by the devilish ones in our crowd.

Grover Hayes

Grover Hayes was in my high school class and through our hunting and boating attractions we became fast friends and played six-man football for Three Forks, Montana High School. Our team was very good and won the State Championship two years in a row. Grover was very fast on his feet and tough. As a halfback he scored many points. One time when we were out duck hunting I borrowed one of his antique, hammer type, double-barreled shotguns and as we were stalking some ducks in a stand of cattails a duck flew out just as I was letting the hammer down the gun went off from the hip and killed the duck. "Damn you're fast" he his said, as I nursed my skinned up knuckles. It wasn't until over fifty years later that I told him that it was a hunter error and unintentional.

Grover had a heavy boat named the "Kubiac Kid" which we took up to Hebgen Lake near Ennis, Montana and after a scoreless day of fishing we were so tired and so weak that we couldn't reload the heavy boat onto the truck. We had to stay overnight to get enough strength to load it early in the morning and then we just barely made it. Our reward was two peanut butter and mustard sandwiches, which were Grover's favorite food. After high school, I lost track of Grove until 1952 when my wife and I renewed acquaintances with him and my other classmate, Harriet (Price,) in Pasadena, California. We lost Grove to a battle with his heart in Y2000 and thank the Lord for the wonderful eulogies that he left with us and for the lasting friendship of my pal Harriet who recently moved from Laguna Beach to San Clemente, California

The Sheriff's Daughter

Connie Helm was another classmate so she became good friends with Grover Hayes as well. Her father E.R. Helm was the sheriff of Trident but was not to be feared. One late night when Grover and I were at Connie's house playing cards and cracking walnut shells on the kitchen table where E.R. [his nick name] had his breakfast of Wheaties all laid out for the morning. His false teeth were neatly soaking in a glass of water and his Wheaties were in a bowl waiting for the newspaper, cream and sugar. If you haven't already guessed, the sneaky trio thought up a prank to play on E.R., so we mixed the walnut shells in with the Wheaties and went home. The next morning when E.R. was blindly reading the newspaper, he chomped into his Wheaties, without his teeth and cut his gums. The walls came down and Connie got blistered while ole Grover and George peacefully slept in at home. From that time on, we were not exactly favorites of sheriff Helm.

Mister Ward

Wherever a group of kids were seen sitting on the ground or around a big Abraham Lincoln type of a man, it was because Mister Ward was in the midst of us spinning yarns in his soft-spoken twanging ways and doing a shuffling kind of tap dance without taps. In spite of his lanky figure and baggy pants he kept us spellbound and entertained us with little moral stories. On the Fourth of July he was always dressed as Uncle Sam with his bushy eyebrows, beard, top hat and extra long legs. These images led us to make stilts to emulate his stature. When Mr. Ward moved to Logan the whole town greatly missed him.

Hap and Lil Gates

Happy [Hap] and Lilly [Lil] Gates lived in an apartment house back of the hotel with their beige Labrador dog. They were a very quiet couple and liked kids. Bill Burkett and I spent many evenings with them playing cards and learning how to sew, to knit and to darn sox. The dog was one of our favorites that loved the water in any kind of weather.

Happy was an expert whitefish fisherman and used to take me with him to all of his favorite riffles and holes on the many rivers around Trident, Logan and Three Forks. He taught me how to make a smoker and how to cure and smoke whitefish, which was one of our staples for food. Smoked whitefish has no equal when done right and keeps without refrigeration for a long time. My father learned how to smoke fish also and when we moved to Logan he became very proficient at it and popular, as well.

One of the things that Happy Gates was noted for was for sawing wood with a three-foot diameter circular saw that was ingeniously driven with the back wheels of his pickup truck and a swing table. One had to be very careful with this open blade whirring at 150 RPM. It was especially risky when sawing old railroad ties for wood or fence posts and timber with nails because a tooth might break or chip by hitting a nail or rock and come flying out at the operator. Two men could cut several cords [4'x4'x8'] of cottonwood in a day. Helping Hap cut wood for other people was quite a learning experience.

Dirty Japs

Because of my parents' Americanized ways, we siblings were raised to be Americans instead of Japanese. This upbringing, that was instilled in us was so valuable and yet so unappreciated until Pearl Harbor drastically changed our identity and we became "Dirty Japs." Sure, along the way we had our share of slurs and kids' kind of stuff, but the real people of Trident prevailed. There wasn't a person or kid that my parents' lives didn't touch in some good way and they were respected for that.

The Oiye siblings were exactly like all of the other siblings and grew up not knowing that we were supposed to be poor or un-American. We had fun making do, playing with bottle caps, marbles, chalk and hopscotch, jumping rope, we had patches on patches, cardboard soles in our worn out shoes, milk can horseshoes, jump ropes made from six little pieces of discarded rope, clamp on roller skates, barrel stave skis, willow fishing poles, third and fourth hand-me-downs, apple box scooters with roller skate wheels, stilts made from two by fours and a leather strap, tobacco can worm cans, willow sling shots, inner tube rubber guns, snake grass whistles, thread spool tic-tacs, rope swings, ice skate runners for ice boats, willow bow and arrows, choke cherry bows, cedar plaques, milk bottle caps, acetylene bombs, string and can telephones, worm vibrators, playing kick the can, snipe hunting, bent over shoe nails that snagged your socks and blistered your feet, and clamp on ice skates that wrecked your shoes. Who hasn't practiced stropping a straight razor and nicking or cutting dad's razor strop that ultimately landed on a bare behind?

Arson

A huge black cloud of smoke and flame came shooting up into the sky along the railroad tracks by the pool hall when I lit a match to some six-foot tall dry Johnson grass that thrived there. My mom happened to be out in front of our house and came running with wet gunny sacks to help beat the fire out. Every other swat that the fire got, I caught, along with a few Japanese words. Arson was never in my bag of tricks again after seeing how scared and black and dirty she was. If nothing else the fire sure did clean out the ditch along the railroad track and eliminate the fire hazard to the pool hall.

Cutworms

Cutworms were a common enemy of the fresh lush back-yard and community gardens. Wherever white butter-flies were hovering over the garden one could be sure that the cutworms would be there. Lettuce, young cabbage, beets, turnips, and especially Chinese cabbage were very vulnerable to the voracious chewers. My sister Peggy and I used to help my mom and dad look for cutworms early in the mornings when the dew was still dripping from the plants. Peg and I particularly had a dislike for Chinese cabbage called nappa in Japanese, so we took advantage of the sneaky opportunity to take the butcher knife and neatly slice off the roots of the young nappa plants. We lied and told our mom that the cutworms did it and she trusted our report. Dad just replanted more to replace them. The truth didn't come out until years later when we started to acquire a taste for nappa in many forms such as [Kim Chee, a Korean pickle] and we still laugh about the learning curve.

Daily Chores

Peggy and Anita and I had many chores to do, like help-ing in the kitchen, hauling coal and wood, cleaning out ashes, mowing lawns, yard and garden work, doing dishes, helping with the laundry making beds and cleaning house. This was part of a normal day and one of our favorite things to do was to save the Del Monte dill pickle juice and drink it as our reward for doing the dishes. Peg washed the dishes while Anita cleared the table and put the dishes away.

My job was always wiping dishes with the homemade dish-towels that mom sewed and embroidered from plain flour sacks.

Mom's Miracle

Mom needed all of the help that she could get from the siblings because she took in laundry and hand washed it until she earned enough money to buy a used square aluminum tub Maytag washing machine. The wringer had a safety bar feature that would automatically trip if you got a finger or arm caught in the wringer or if the ladies got their hair wound up in the rollers. This was an excellent feature and saved all of us at one time or another fom being seriously hurt. Many a long night mom ironed clothes or stayed up sewing or mending all of our wardrobes. Anita spent many nights rubbing and massaging mom's back and shoulders that gave her a lot of pain and discomfort until she was miraculously healed by a bite from a rattle snake while she pulled weeds from her beautiful flower garden.

Pop

Pop needed all of the help that he could get to do the gardening and woodcutting because the growing season without frost was barely ninety days long and the soil was all worked by hand. He gathered and cut firewood from railroad ties, cottonwood trees, willow bushes, dried up juniper cedar trees, old boxes and anything else that would burn. Repairing the old second hand 1923 Chevrolet touring car, that he bought for seventy five dollars in 1930, took many hours keeping the tires patched, side curtains replaced, unplugging the fuel system, replacing stripped gears and broken axles, replacing plate glass windshields, changing spark plugs and oil every thousand miles and even overhauling the engine every twenty thousand miles or sooner if the power diminished to a chug and a backfire. Next came the repairing of shoes to make them last until the leather tops completely wore out and wouldn't hold nails or sewing any more. Canning time was a busy time harvesting and processing fruits and vegetables while mom cooked and canned. That unforgettable smell comes back with every trip to the super market.

Eight year old, George's hands-on learning experience was quite vivid and valuable but, not always so helpful to my dad. Tom's inimitable patience as a teacher and a father exposed me to real life, where the rubber meets the road, at an early age to be resourceful and to find ways to make do. I was a menace, when it came to learning how to use and to sharpen tools though. If my son, Tom had invented ways not to use tools as I did, I'm sure that one of us wouldn't be here today. My father's basement and garage showed signs or footprints of misused tools that I claimed weren't mine. I think that my dad's life would have been a lot more simple and peaceful if I would have been a girl; but then my mom would have had more problems to deal with.

Benny

In the Japanese culture the baby in the family enjoys all of the privileges of a prince or princess and is the adored one with no chores to do. Brother Ben fit into that role very nicely and became adored by the whole town. He developed a humorous and friendly personality that follows him though his life today.

Scotty Irvin

That's an earthquake sky! Were the warning words that old Scotty Irvin used to use to intimidate everyone in town. Although Scotty lived in WOP town, he was not of Italian origin, so he must have been one of those nationals that came with out papers. He was a short, slightly built, Scotsman philosopher who had silver white hair and looked old to the kids. He used to wander over into town and to get our attention; he would point his skinny forefinger to the sky and in a shaky voice say, *"Better watch out! That's an earthquake sky!"* All of a sudden things seemed to get spooky and it felt like a cool wind blowing. When our skin got goose bumps and our hair stood on end, we'd run home and hide under the bed to keep from getting hurt in the earthquake. Of course nothing ever happened except in our little naïve minds. Scotty lived in a corrugated tin shack and had a crystal radio, which added to his mystique. I don't remember if he ever worked in the cement factory but he was usually seen going over the dump and along the railroad tracks.

Old Bill Sumner

Bill Sumner, an unusual man with a large, bulbous, deeply pocked marked nose, lived next door to us and the pool hall/barber shop. He was a brutishly built man and when he wore his buffalo skin coat in the winter, he was rather frightening to see.

Old Bill was the barber, bartender and ran the pool hall. He had a Model T Ford touring car that sat out in his back yard near our yard. We could see him brush off the snow and go through the motions of starting it. When he set the spark lever too far in the advanced position, the engine would huff and puff as he hand cranked it, like a big old buffalo trying to mate with the car; then all of a sudden the engine would kick and old Bill would go flying though the air and land in a snow bank. The cussing and swearing that he spouted off were all new to me and I was instructed to not use those words even though they were never forgotten.

I got my first store bought hair cut from Bill and my neck and ears still remember those big, cold, hand-clippers that pulled like mad. My father did a much better job with his cheap clippers. If I didn't sit still, which was hard to do because I itched so much, without warning, he would hit me on top of the head with the clippers. Can you imagine trying to give a turtle a hair cut with his neck drawn in as far as it would retract and he slid down so far in the chair that his head was on the seat? There were no more barbershop haircuts in Bill's place for me.

Floyd Sumner

Bill's son Floyd, about five years my senior, used to entice me to sneak into the pool hall and show me his dad's guns. One day he was showing me how to load his dad's 30.06 hunting rifle; we were standing behind the bar where all of the dishes were stacked and as he closed the bolt, the gun went off and a whole bunch of dishes fell on the floor and broke. Fortunately, the gun was pointed at the floor and it only shot a hole in the flooring. The sound was deafening inside of the building so we quickly put the gun away, swept up the broken dishes, and ran like heck. Floyd of course made up some sort of a lie when old Bill Sumner found out about it and set up a fusillade of foul language that sounds like what happens when you poke sticks at penned up animals.

Fishing on the Madison

Fishing on the Madison River was a wonderful source of food and recreation for my dad and from the time that I was seven years old he would take me with him. We would get up about three o'clock in the morning after having spent all evening getting ready and then restlessly waiting for the alarm to ring. We had a big breakfast of oatmeal, pancakes, eggs and coffee and then packed a lunch of two fried egg sandwiches and an apple. Our boots, fishing poles, fishing-reels, line, leaders, hooks and a bait-net were already loaded into the old 1923 model Chevrolet touring car. We were off for the long [15 mile] drive up the rutted gumbo road on the lower Madison road to any one of the farm houses from the Wilcox's to the Bate's place.

The first stop would be to catch minnows, for bait, in the irrigation ditch that ran along the road. It was very important to keep the bait as fresh as possible and better yet alive. We tried to be on the water by daybreak and walking in our boots, carrying all of our fishing gear and baskets, was quite invigorating for our short legs.

That first cast along a big boulder forming a hole is an excitement only a fisherman can feel or anticipate. When that big rainbow or brown trout makes a lunge for the bait it is like an electrifying moment of win or lose. Will the tackle be strong enough, did the fish get hooked well, is the line long enough, how big is he, where do I land it and all of these thoughts get integrated and processed before the catch is made? After falling into the river a couple of times during the catch was to be expected and hip boots were often exchanged for overalls and tennis shoes. Just shivering in the cold morning air waiting for the sun to come out seemed like an eternity but such fun and worth it, especially when the total catch was measured by the size of mom's washtub.

Even sitting on the bank eating a soggy, wet, fried-egg sandwich seemed like heaven. With all of the modern high tech fishing equipment, SUV cars, good roads, freezers, ice chests, prepackaged lunches, and float boats; there is nothing that compares with doing it the hard way with bum equipment and lots of big wild fish to test it.

When my dad's fishing hat came floating down the river, this little guy was scared to death and retrieved the hat with all kinds of negative thoughts running through my whole being. After running though the willows and wild rose bushes that snagged my fishing tackle and destroyed it and after falling down a few times, much to my relief, I saw my dad in the riffle upstream fishing away. *As only a seven year old would do, I nonchalantly gave my father his hat and said I rescued it. He said, "Thanks, the wind took it away." How panic could instantly turn to artificial calmness has always been a mystery to me; but it didn't undo the scratched up body and broken fishing gear.*

The long ride home after dark was a test of endurance when the Vacuum tank in the fuel system plugged up and the rotten vacuum hose started to leak. After much taping of the hose with a lot of sucking on the vacuum system we got the car started long enough to have a flat tire in the middle of the gumbo ruts on the Madison road. When we finally got home, mom was always waiting with great anticipation to get the fresh fish. The very next Saturday was a repeat performance.

The Chevy

Our first automobile was a six or seven-year-old, 1923 Chevrolet touring car, which was an experience to behold. It had a steering system that was worn out and the car would shimmy like a wet dog shaking himself, my father would change the bushings and bearings quite often to make it drive smoothly and stay on the road. The steering wheel was unique in that it had a latch on it that would allow fat men to get in and out of the car.

The transmission shifting mechanism was so loose that it was always a prayer and a promise as to whether it would shift into the proper gear. Many times it would shift into reverse instead of second gear and all of the gear teeth on the ring and pinion gear would get wiped out or the rear axel would break. Everyone got a whiplash, which was called a stiff neck in those days.

George at ten years of age, would ride the Northern Pacific local train called the "Stub," sixty miles to Helena from Trident and the Ogata boys, Gen and Dye would take me to the junk yard to buy new/used parts and return home the same day. That was a learning experience in many walks of life and I grew up pretty fast. One time I even had to go to the Barnum and Bailey Circus to get an axle with the right model gear because the circuses used car axles for tent pegs and the junkyard didn't have the right one.

To be covered with grease from head to toe was some kind of a big boys status symbol, so George, much to mom's chagrin, got a lot of clothes greasy but Fels Naptha bar soap would somehow miraculously get them clean.

In spite of the shortcomings of the old Chevy, my mom and dad bravely and naively took us four siblings on long camping trips to Meadow Creek, Bear Trap, Karst Kamp, Bozeman Hot Springs, Yellowstone Park, Potosi Hot Springs, and up the west side of the Madison River to Green's Ranch, all of which are not easily accessed even with modern SUV's. All of that required driving over steep mountain-passes, wet rutted roads, and boulder-strewn trails. On many occasions the radiator would boil over and we would be precariously hanging on the shoulder of the road, with rocks under the wheels to keep us from rolling down the 2000 or 3000-foot grade, while our parents walked to the bottom of the grade for water. Or, maybe it was a flat tire, a broken fan belt or a broken axel. One time as we were driving down the road, the rear wheel passed us up while we skidded to halt in an alfalfa field, next to an irrigation ditch. An axel had broken and the rear wheel came off and went for an unattached ride.

The Ogata Family

In 1934 when I was twelve years old, my father taught me how to drive the old Chevy and would let me do quite a bit of the driving when we went fishing and wood gathering. In that same year, when school was out in May, Mr. Ogata needed some help on his expanding truck farm in Helena, Montana, so my father sent me off to help out for $1.00 per day (16 hours) with board and room. It was an eye-opener for me to have to learn no nonsense, big time vegetable farming as a business.

Gen Ogata, the oldest son was preparing to enter college at Bozeman to learn Agriculture and the second son Dye Ogata, was looking at greener pastures elsewhere, so they welcomed my coming on board. Martha the oldest daughter took care of all of the domestic chores along with her sister Yeiko and Fumi, while their mother and young John tended the gardening work. Hoover, the baby of the family, enjoyed being the crown prince, so to speak and just played.

I was given a small tar papered room in the Japanese Railroad Camp along the railroad tracks where raw steam was piped over from the nearby roundhouse to provide our hot water and heating. The first week was rather frightening and I got my first taste of being homesick, not a good feeling.

Gen immediately started to teach me, how to make out sales slips, to drive the sales route in Helena, Montana, how to peddle vegetables, how to take orders, how to build up display stands, how to collect money and how to manage double entry bookkeeping. Dye and Johnny taught me how to use all of the farm machinery and equipment and to keep it repaired. Mrs. Ogata, Martha, Yeiko and Fumi taught me how to hoe, cultivate long rows of veggies, to harvest veggies, to wash and bunch veggies, to put up orders and to sort potatoes.

Our days started at daybreak, which was about 5:00 AM and ended at dark, which was 9:00 or 10:00 PM in Montana. Mr. Ogata taught me all about the fine art of raising good vegetables, mass production methods, and how to handle Indians, who lived in teepees in the fields and provided the heavy labor if I could get them to work. To give me identity and status right away, I had to buy blue and white-stripped bib-overalls just like the ones that Gen and Dye wore, while other farmers wore blue denims. I even had to learn to swagger a little.

Driver Training

The city of Helena, Montana is built in the creek bed of Last Chance Gulch, one of the richest places in Montana during the gold rush days, its only equal being Alder Gulch at Virginia City. It's main street went up and down a very narrow canyon and was just wide enough for a double street car track, double parallel parking for cars and business houses along the side walk. Automobiles had to share the same roadbed as the streetcars and made driving very risky. Every two blocks was a side street that went up the steep sides of the canyon with stores along the sides.

On my first solo run to deliver a load of produce to the stores in Helena, I had to go to one of the Brackman Stores, that was located about half a block up-hill on the right hand curb of the first side street, so I parked our rickety old homemade Chevy pickup truck there and went into the store. When I came out of the store, the truck and its load of produce was gone. At the bottom of the hill at the intersection with Main Street was a lot of commotion and a lot of police cars and a fire truck were there. It seems that, much to my chagrin, my truck had lost its brakes, crossed the intersection and ran backwards into the entrance of the bank building on that corner. No one was hurt except my big ego and Mr. Ogata's pocketbook for the repair costs of the granite fascia front of the bank. *That took a lot of veggies at 25 cents for a dozen large bunches to pay for the damages incurred. Mr. Ogata graciously let me off of the hook.*

One would think that Mr. Ogata would have sent me home, but with his big grin he sent me out again. This time everything went okay at the first Brackman store but, at the second Brackman store, which was located on the next block over, heading downhill to Main Street and on the right hand curb, I came down the hill a little too fast and the brakes didn't hold. The truck jumped the curb and this time it went through the plate glass front of the store. Naturally there was more chagrin and expenses to pay for the plate glass window. The amazing part was that I still didn't get fired. I grew a lot and Mr. Ogata got poorer.

The next week I made a delivery to the Safeway store on Main Street and double parallel parked such that the truck was on the streetcar track. I wasn't strong enough to lift a hundred pound sack of potatoes off of the truck, so I stood the sack upright and got down on the ground and tipped the potato sack on to my shoulder. After wobbling a few steps I fell down and the potatoes came down on top of me, pinning me to the streetcar tracks. Clang, clang, clang came the streetcar. The conductor got out and carried the potatoes into the store while everyone roared. I might have even cried a little, but the good news is that, by the end of the summer, this skinny little kid could lift a hundred pound sack of potatoes over my head and load a boxcar. Yes, and even drive in Helena, Montana.

By the end of the summer Mr. Ogata bought a new pickup truck and sent me home with a sack of potatoes, a sack of rice, a sack of flour, and a sack of sugar for my father, so that I wouldn't spend the money. I did buy my school clothes, though.

In the second year 1935, that I worked for Mr. Ogata I became quite skilled at the truck farming business and was a good driver, an excellent bookkeeper, a good salesman, a good mechanic and equipment operator from cultivators to diesel caterpillars. I had earned enough money to buy a real good Kodak Model 620 folding camera with a good lens and shutter adjustments. I even became a good photographer. Those were important footprints in my life.

Model-A Ford

In 1936, Mr. Koga, our Japanese friend from Three Forks, sold Tom his 1932 Model-A Ford deluxe sedan for $75.00.

From then on the fuel system problems, bad tires, broken fan belts, broken axles, transmission shifting problems, skinned knuckles, side curtain and canvas top replacements, exhaust fumes, all went away and a real heater replaced the hot bricks that kept us warm in the winter. *Such luxury!*

In the summer of 1936, at the age of fourteen I got a better paying job working with my dad at the cement factory in Trident. In 1937 I got my Social Security Number when they first came out that year.

The fall of 1936 was also a new beginning for me when I started High school in Three Forks. High school was a time of new awakenings, new challenges, new friends, experimentation with life, testing of ones aspirations, and a strong desire to break away from the shelter of parents. So for two years I was getting into mischief and stretching the boundaries at school and within the environs of Trident.

School Bus Driver

George Demosco, was our school bus driver to Three Forks from Trident. Before he got a brand new factory made blue bus with cross rows of seats and an aisle down the middle; he had an old homegrown, long, narrow bus with two rows of benches along the sides and an entry door with steps at the back. He had a lever at the front that he could open and close the back door. This old bus had a long overhang from the back wheels so with a little bouncing on the steps; the front wheels would come off of the ground. When conditions like that exist and teen age school boys get to feeling their oats; we all moved to the back of the bus including girls and got out on the step and on the roof and started jumping. Before Mr. Demosco could stop the bus, the front wheels came off of the ground and we landed in the ditch near the bend at Fort Rock. Miraculously, no one was hurt when the bus came back down after some of us fell off of the roof and it got back on the road. Mr. Demosco was such a good sport; he never did turn us in to the authorities or to our parents.

CHAPTER 3

Logan, Montana
[1938-1947]

L ogan, Montana was a little railroad town nestled on the south side of a bend in the Gallatin River about a quarter of a mile wide and a half of mile long between two cliffs. The Northern Pacific Railroad Company had a terminal here complete with a roundhouse, coal dock, water tank, icehouse, sand house, depot with a beanery, and twelve sidetracks that made up the railroad yard.

At Logan, trains coming from Bozeman to the east were divided and ran on both sides of the river. Trains continuing west went to Butte via Three Forks, Willow Creek and Whitehall on the south side of the Jefferson River. Trains heading north to Helena and Great Falls went on the north side of the Missouri River via an open span bridge at the extreme west end of town.

The Truck Farm

*G*ather up all of the family assets, including the piggy banks, we're going to buy a twenty three acre truck *farm in Logan, Montana for twenty three hundred dollars were the words of Tom and Taka in the summer of 1938. Both girls had gone off to college and were no longer living at home, so Ben and I came up with about $300 to add to the pot. Since the Exclusion Act prevented my parents from owning land, my name was used to go on the deed because I was a natural born American citizen.*

This property was located on the west edge of Logan across the Railroad Bridge on the road to Helena, via Trident, six or seven miles north along the Gallatin River. The river and the railroad tracks provided the property lines bounding the twenty-three acres of bottomland. Cottonwood trees lined the riverbank and served as a barrier to keep the river from washing the banks away. However, the trees were very vulnerable to the abundant quantity of industrious beaver and had to be constantly protected.

At the railroad bridge was a deep hole along the willow-lined bank of the Gallatin River which made an ideal place for a small "Hobo Jungle," At the lower end of the property, where the river turned ninety degrees into the railroad tracks was another deep swirling hole in the river, with lots of fish. Several beaver dams and a cotton-wooded island in the river added to the excellent fishing holes and places for ducks and pheasants to hide. A country road with an iron-framed bridge crossing the river split the property into two parcels of land, seven acres and sixteen acres of which about twenty acres was cultivable.

This farm was known as the Old Boomer Place and was owned by Henry Raymond, a big time cabbage grower, when we bought it. The road split at the railroad tracks and went either to the horseshoe hills or to Trident. Until a bridge was built across the Gallatin River at Trident, this was the only road to Trident from Three Forks.

What better conditions could there be for a "Hobo Jungle" than a railroad track, a river, lots of fish and a vegetable farm with willows and with lots of cottonwood trees? Fence posts also made excellent firewood. The Oiye's soon learned that a hobo was a real person struggling to find a living and my mom was their best friend and my dad didn't see the garden diminishing or the fence posts having to be replaced. Our dog Buster, a German shepherd, had other ideas though and wouldn't let them near our house.

Farm Equipment

First came our "Monkey" Wards 5-HP garden Tractor to supplement the Ford-Ferguson tractor that came with the farm. The Ford tractor was a great machine for truck farming; but was no match for the John Deere Farmall tractor which was much more versatile and faster. However, the little Ward's two-wheel, walk-behind, cultivator tractor made up for the Ford tractors shortcomings and did a lot of work on a very small amount of fuel.

The Whisky Still

Of interest was the fact that our water well had the best tasting water of any well around Logan and during the prohibition days the water made good booze. It seems that under the house in the basement and root cellar the bootleggers had a whiskey-still. They pumped water from the river for the boiler and got good water from the well for the booze. We were told that the way in which they got caught was when the revenuers saw the pigs staggering around the yard because they were drunk from eating the mash used for the moonshine.

Irrigation Water

The farm had to get its irrigation water by bringing it down along the north shore of the Gallatin River by an irrigation ditch that started at a beaver dam about a quarter of a mile above the town of Logan. The river water had to be brought down about a half of a mile along a steep mountain sidewall before arriving at the farm. On a good day, about three hundred inches of water at the dam was half of that by the time that it got to the farm. The problems of bringing the water down the ditch ranged from rock slides diverting the water back to the river, beavers and muskrats digging holes in the banks, willows growing in and over the ditch, spring floods washing the banks out, rock slides, dams washing out, hobos breaking down the banks, and low water in the river.

Until the later years, when we installed a pump at the railroad bridge, my brother Ben and I spent a lot of time keeping the ditch repaired. We built concrete dams at the head gate and even tiled about two hundred yards of the ditch with fifty five gallon oil barrel-halves that we had split with a chisel and sledge hammer. All of the materials had to be ferried across the river in my little home made kayak, but it worked.

A Sixteen-Year-Old Man

I was sixteen years old when we moved to Logan and my fun times playing with the Burkett's, Grover Hayes, and the Trident kids came to a sudden halt and hauling manure, plowing, re-grading the land, killing weeds and gophers, and repairing the irrigation system *fell* on my shoulders so that my father could continue working at the cement plant at Trident. My father worked on the farm before he went to work at Trident and after he got home from work. We all worked hard getting the farm in order and of course my mom spent from dawn to dusk working the fields, as well.

When most young men get into high school their curiosities turn to girls and socializing. In the oriental culture it was not appropriate to demonstrate any affection by overt physical contact and to further help make it unacceptable, mixed marriages were frowned upon. In some states in America it was illegal for Caucasians to marry Orientals, so with these kinds of cultural barriers existing, it made working on the farm a convenient place to dispel pent up emotions of being on the outside looking in. Like my parents, any affection or emotion for the opposite sex was an embarrassment for me even though nature would have preferred it to be normal. Until I married a Japanese American girl with a similar background and also until I became a Christian did overtly hugging women and especially men, become a normal and desirable thing to do. I have included this little snippet into my autobiography, in this chapter, to give the reader some idea and understanding of what made Sammy run during the shaping of my real culture.

Madam Laura

Whenever times got dull around our house or during the occasions when the family and close friends were gathered together, my mom used to get the biggest charge out of telling the story about selling veggies to flaming red haired, "Madam Laura." It seems that when Laura was ready to pay for her purchases, she would hike up her dress, roll down her rayon stocking and pull out a huge wad of cash without batting an eye, much to mom's surprise and embarrassment, especially if other customers were there. Laura always handed her a big $10.00 bill for $2.00 worth of veggies that took all of mom's small bills to make change. It was an eye opener for me to see how scrawny her legs were. At the end of the day or on a Sunday, mom would have second thoughts about taking that kind of money or putting it in the offering plate at church. We had many discussions about that and concluded that cash has no conscience.

The Green House

A lean-to, glass green house that was attached to the garage and coal shed served to raise tomato plants, cabbage plants, lettuce plants, celery plants, cucumber plants onion sets, and broccoli plants to extend the frost free season a few weeks. During the off season in the late fall and winter, the green house required a lot of maintenance replacing glass, re-glazing windows, hauling in new topsoil and organic fertilizer, repairing the water system, repairing the heating system, and etc.

We also had glass and gauze or screen covered seeding beds for raising plants for transplanting. By May and June the ground would start to thaw out and our field would be rowed into three foot wide hills and the plants would be set out, one at a time, under wax paper Hot Caps that served as little individual green houses until the frost was over. Sometime it snowed on the Fourth of July and it was a toss-up as to whether the plants would survive.

The Salad Bowl

In 1939 we had the most beautiful crop of everything growing and looking the best that it could, when a sixty or seventy mile per hour, driving hail storm came out of nowhere and leveled our gold mine of six months of struggling, backbreaking labor and turned it into a salad bowl within a few minutes. Almost all of the glass in the green house needed replacement.

Undaunted Courage

Stephen Ambrose wrote a book called "Undaunted Courage," that describes how tough the men and Sacajawea, of the Lewis and Clark Expedition were to succeed. My parents' strong will to succeed, when we plowed it all under to try it again, while their tears ran on the inside so they didn't show on the outside, was a good example of the same kind of character that helped build this country that he wrote about.

What's Next For Me?

Now that there were no more crops to tend until next year, I went to work on Tom Koga's extra gang to earn survival money and became an expert spiker. John Satake, from Harlowtown, Montana, Mr. Koga's assistant foreman, became my very dear friend and taught me all about building a railroad and helped me to endure the rigors of railroading and life. My muscle tones increased even more and the heavy work toughened me up for two years of championship football at Three Forks High School. Ironically John and I fought together during the rescue of the lost battalion in WWII in the Vosges Mountains in France.

State Football Champions

WOW! To be on the first Southern Montana State Championship six-man football team at TFHS. To be the classmate, quarterback co-captain with the famous Colonel Dean Pogreba leaves one with wonderful and priceless historical moments and flashbacks. Coach Nobel Stevenson and teammates like Dean Pogreba, Yokichi Itoh, Robert Itoh, Wally Lane, Pete Kolokatrone, Paul Haigh, Guido Ferris, Frank Parr, Dick Spoonmore, Jack Roadarmel,

Bill Roadarmel, Gene Burns, Bruce Batchelder, Grover Hayes, and Bob Ruggles are faces that I see every time that I watch a football game. That was a lot of fun, especially beating Wilsal, Montana, 119 to zero and tackling Big Bill Wheat from Sheridan, Montana

Mrs. Koga

During the time when I was working on the extra gang , for some reason I had to be in the kitchen car helping Jack the cook prepare dinner of fried fish. In those days, everything was pan fried in lard or bacon grease. The extra gang was usually located on some remote siding, a long ways from civilization, so the common practice was to toss all garbage out the door and down the railroad embankment. The wild animals usually cleaned up most of the edibles so it was sort of crudely self-policing. On this particular summer day, Jack had just finished cooking a batch of fish and tossed the dripping pan full of hot grease out the door. There was an earth shaking scream as the grease hit Mr. Koga's daughter, May right on top of the head and knocked her to the ground. Mrs. Koga, who was with May, picked her up and started shouting for us to bring butter, which we did, then came ice water and towels and blankets to calm May from the shock.

To this day, I don't think I have ever witnessed anything so shocking and so bravely and efficiently managed, as Mrs. Koga's heroism in saving her daughter from being scarred and disfigured for life. Last summer, I visited May and we relived that crisis. What a miracle it was that she survived without a scar, when sheets of skin fell off of her shoulders, her hair fell out and her face was all blistered. Today, butter is not an acceptable procedure for applying to a burn so it must have been the ice water and God that did the job.

The Big Tee

In the spring of 1940 our senior class voted to give the school a gift of a letter on the hill west of town near the Jefferson river. We decided to outdo Montana State College, who had the world's largest blocked in letter, so we hired a surveyor to layout the Tee with an Eff incorporated in the stem for Three Forks. When the day came to do the job, the twenty three men and women students in our class started out early one Saturday morning armed with picks, shovels, gloves, buckets, rakes, white wash and brooms, thinking that it would be a piece of cake. The hill that we chose was covered with sagebrush and cactus and was so steep that it was hard to keep from sliding downhill. When we started to clear the sagebrush out and pile rocks to be whitewashed, we discovered that we had eyes much bigger than our heads, we decided on the spot to dig a trench two feet wide on the out line and to cover it with rocks.

While the guys did the digging and hauling rocks the gals did the whitewashing until we killed a few rattlesnakes. They hurriedly slopped the whitewash on and got most of it on us guys every chance that they got.

It was late in the day when we finished the job and we were filthy dirty and covered with whitewash, so we headed to the Jefferson River and either jumped in or got thrown in. It's amazing that we survived that crazy idea. The Tee-Eff looked out of proportion and several years later one of the other classes re-modeled the letter to just a Tee and much shorter in height as it stands today. So much for that pipe dream!

Expelled

It is not a very well known fact that several of us in the same senior class got kicked out of school. Three weeks prior to graduation, we almost didn't graduate because we couldn't raise enough money, eighty-eight cents each for a little crime that we committed while on a field trip. To protect the criminals, their names are not mentioned.

About six of us guys and gals were in Mr. Shearsons' geology class and he arranged, with the school board chairman to let his class visit an old abandoned gold mine on his sheep ranch, located on the North Bench near Three Forks. We thought that that was a neat idea since he wasn't coming along and we could have fun. All of us piled into one of our classmates Model A Ford Roadster and found our way to the sheep ranch. A little ways past the first gate we came to an old dilapidated shed with some windows in it so, one of the gals said Stop! Stop! And proceeded to find a rock and wound up and threw it at the windows. Wow! The rock hit a cross member and broke half of the thirty or so windows. The guys couldn't stand to see that happen and we all threw rocks until all of the windows were broken. From there we went to the gold mine but didn't go in because it was caving in and there were rattlesnakes down there so we drove back to town and dispersed.

Bright and early the next day, we were met with a stern faced principal, Mr. Shearson who said that we were expelled from school until we replaced all of the windows in the Chairman's lambing shed. We all acted innocent as he proceeded to inform us that there was a sheepherder behind the shed that witnessed all of this and while we were at the mine he reported us.

What to do? The Trident bunch didn't have a problem because they rode the school bus and so did the Logan bunch. Therefore, the parents didn't know that they were not in school. It seems that the guys had enough money to go to the pool hall and play pool all day or to the roller skating hall, but didn't have eighty-eight cents to spare for the glass and the gals were sweating it out.

The Oiye's were in the process of re-glassing their green house in Logan and a box full of glass mysteriously disappeared.

We were eight pieces of glass short and time was running out to graduation day. One night we all went to the roller skating hall and discovered that the big bay window on the backside of the building had a sheet of glass waiting to be replaced. Calculating, we figured that we could cut it into eight panes of the right size. It was kind of strange watching that pane of glass slide along the wall a little bit at a time as the crowd skated in a circle. Once out the door during a lot of commotion, the glass was taken to a lumberyard where another classmate skillfully cut it up for us.

Just in time we paid our debt and graduated, one of us gave the salutatory speech, while moms and dads clapped. Crime does pay!

One-year Sabbatical

Following graduation from High school in 1940, I stayed out of school for a year to work the farm, to sell vegetables and to earn money to go to college. Jack Roadarmel, my classmate, did likewise. My brother Ben's days of being the favored youngest one ended also and we spent a lot of days and late nights working the ditches and harvesting veggies. I drove to Three Forks, Manhattan, Belgrade, Helena, Bozeman, and Livingston selling our veggies, while my Mom and Ben sold from the fields. If we sold fifty dollars worth in a day, it was a good day.

The Power of God

Lightning and crashing thunderstorms are common in Montana, and some nights look as bright as day when a tree, a transformer, or a prominent point is the target for literally the hair-raising discharge of millions of volts of highly ionized air.

One time when I was getting out of our pick-up truck in front of the Logan store and post office, a bolt of lightning hit a transformer on the other side of the river about 150 yards away. Just as I stepped into a puddle of water I got hit by a small portion of the main blast and thrown to the ground.

Mr. [Little Joe] MacQuillan ran out of the store and dragged me to safety. The only thing that happened to me was a few bruises and a very shaken up wet young man.

By sheer accident, I once took a picture with my Brownie camera, of lightning striking a power pole in our back yard by leaving the shutter open for a log time during an electrical storm that we were having. It was awesome to see the dendrites of lightning lashing out so close to our house.

Northern Lights

Even more hair-raising than being inside of a Montana style lightning and thunder storm is to witness on a clear, cold, winter night, what is called an Aurora Borealis or commonly known as Northern Lights.

This is a soundless, luminous geomagnetic phenomenon of shooting light streaks piercing the outer universe or arches of colored lights that light up the arctic regions of the sky. The sight is almost indescribable and must be experienced more than just witnessed or heard about or studied about to get the sensations and feelings that accompany the occurrence. *No matter how many times that I have had that not to forget experience, my awe of God's power and immensity only increases.*

A Batch of Pigs!

Bruce (Batch) Batchelder, the youngest of the two Batchelder boys teamed up with my brother and me in a hog raising venture along the river bank on our farm that provided us with some riotous fun. We bought ten six week old shoats from Jimmy Lane, the butcher in Three Forks, for about $2.50 each and we got the excess buttermilk from the Batchelder creamery in Three Forks to feed them. The little shoats weighed about five to ten pounds each in the early spring and were slick and pinkish in color with smiling faces and sharp upright ears some with black and white spots.

They could run as fast as a race horse and had to be tackled a lot to catch the big males for castrating or when they got out of the sty and ran away. Since we were both on the football team, tackling piglets was better practice than playing football and Bruce with his ear-to-ear grin was a sight to remember, especially when the pigs tackled him or me. Ben being smaller got his share of chasing loose pigs and getting banged around by them, as well. These funny little guys became more like pets than a business.

The Manhattan Grain Elevator staff was very nice to us and allowed us to sweep up under the grain chutes and places where the grain leaked out of the main storage bins and elevators. They also gave us steam rolled oats for practically nothing. We mixed this grain in a fifty-five gallon oil drum filled with boiling hot buttermilk and made a mash for feed. The pigs loved the mixture and went around with squeaky smiles on their faces all day long.

Every month a traveling salesman from the Watkins Company visited our farm to sell us farmer type of remedies and food supplements for animals. He saw our pigs and said that the pigs needed minerals to supplement their diet for them to put on weight faster, which we were striving to do. Our goal was to have our pigs weighing the ideal weight of 225 lbs, by October but we couldn't afford to buy the minerals.

The salesman was a nice man and had a soft heart for the three entrepreneurs and said *"I will let you in on a little secret if you have any slack coal."* He proceeded to tell us that slack coal would do the same job as his minerals and that the pigs loved it. We didn't believe him but when we saw those pigs going around the yard crunching on lumps of coal like a jawbreaker, we exploded with laughter and went around cleaning out other peoples' coal bins and fed it to the pigs just to see that funny sight. It was always something to show to guests and to gloat about. Sometimes though, our pigs got diarrhea when we overdid it and we had unexpected problems to cope with.

When October came around and we were ready for market Jimmy Lane bought most of our prime hogs and our parents and friends bought the rest. Loading those 225 pound hogs into a truck, without having a ramp or loading chute to do it properly was quite an amateurish undertaking. We lost only one pig out of the ten that we started out with. That amounts to 10% of our potential profits. Not having the right tools or equipment sure does bring out the creativity and make-do spirit in one.

When I went to college, Batch became my second quarter college roommate for a short time until he joined a fraternity and later went off to war. Sometime, after the war was over, Bruce went into the pig raising business. It was located out side of Logan on the hillside near the Carpenter Lane turn off. He was in the creamery business in Manhattan at the time and went into this large-scale business in a very sophisticated and modern production way. Much to the Oiye' pleasure, he was very successful in the business that had its roots in our back yard and gave us a lot of joy during the early years of rejection from the war.

Our social life on the farm at Logan, Montana was far

from being sterile. People are really wonderful friends when we let them participate in our lives and we accept them as neighbors.

The Roadarmels

Mrs. Martha Roadarmel faithfully drove a makeshift school bus from Logan to Three Forks that had a leaky exhaust pipe that ran the length of the bus to provide heat in the winter as well as a few scorched legs. The Roadarmel boys, the two Oiye boys and I believe a girl from the Carpenter Lane rode the bus for two years.

The winter months were especially difficult for Mrs. Roadarmel, with arthritis in both hands, to drive down those old rutted country roads; but she cheerfully showed up and I don't remember missing a day of school even at fifty below zero in the snow. The life of a homesteader living on free land didn't come as easy as some people are led to believe. Driving the bus was a small part of what she used to do. Earl Roadarmel Senior had arthritis so bad that he could barely get around so the boys and Mrs. Roadarmel got the job done and we still had time to play and ride horses.

After they came home from church, in the fall months during the hunting season, it was my good fortune to spend almost every Sunday with the Roadarmel's, hunting, fishing, horseback riding and ice-skating. But, best of all was to enjoy Martha's fine farmer cooked meals. Out of her home-steaded farm house kitchen that was without running water or modern conveniences came the most delicious fried pheasants, ducks, geese, rabbits, deer and elk meals that I have ever eaten. Except for my own mom's cooking there was no place that I would rather go for dinner. When you've had a good farmer style meal with lots of meat, mashed potatoes or rice and gravy, and home made bread with hand churned butter topped with homemade jams and jelly, and that sensory pleasure never leaves you.

Earl Roadarmel Sr. in his better days, when I first net him through his boys was quite a beaver trapper and had a mile long boundary to his homestead that bordered on the Gallatin River that was heavily wooded with cottonwood trees and many beaver dams. During the trapping season he was very busy trapping, skinning and drying beaver hides on boards. Although, the beaver were constantly changing the course of the river and doing damage to the land, they provided a reasonable income.

Ducks, geese, deer, coyotes, muskrats, pheasants, and an occasional moose would provide the Roadarmel' s with food during the open seasons and fish from the river were easily caught. Mr. Roadarmel had a ten-gauge lever action shot gun that he was an expert shot with and could bring down a goose at 150 yards in the middle of a grain or alfalfa field, where I couldn't reach them at a hundred yards with my twelve gauge full choke shot gun.

Bill, Earl and I used to really enjoy hunting for pheasants in the cottonwood trees and along their irrigation ditches. Mr. Roadarmel also raised red pigs that did a lot of rooting in the fields and fencerows and required lots of attention, especially when they got into the potato patch.

How to Dry Pick a Turkey

Every Thanksgiving season it was an awesome thing to watch and to participate with the whole Roadarmel family in dry picking turkeys.

Mr. Roadarmel would hang a big bird [twenty pounds or more] by the legs on a rope or trapeze. He would then hang a five to ten-pound weight with a hook on it into the turkey's mouth, while everyone held on to the wings and neck and he would stick an ice pick into the roof of the turkey's mouth and start the blood to drain slowly out of the live bird.

At that moment everyone started frantically pulling wing feathers and large body feathers out before the blood quit flowing and rigor mortise set in. At this time the turkey would have convulsions and start flapping its wings and even a heavy person could be thrown to the ground. If the wing and large body feathers weren't plucked by that time, it was almost impossible to get them out even with a pair if pliers. The trick was to get the job done without bruising the meat in anyway because it affected the price.

This whole operation to this point, took about five minutes or less but, the final plucking and dressing took another half an hour or so. That was literally being picked alive and quite morbid. Today, most turkeys are dunked in hot water like a chicken and mechanically plucked, but in those days some people insisted on dry picked turkeys they claimed tasted better.

Loganites

Little Joe McQuillan also known as Mac and his wife Nonie [Waters] of Manhattan were the first new people that we met in the town of Logan. They ran The Logan Mercantile Co / Post Office and our good friend from Trident, John Madden was the butcher. Little Mac was loved by everyone and in spite of his size he headed up Logan's very good baseball team.

Both Joe and Nonie saw to it that the Oiye's were accepted into the community of Logan.

We already knew the Olson family that came from Trident a few years earlier. Then we met Mr. Johnston, the school principal; the Bill Hendershot's, who ran the beanery; Butch the handyman and auto mechanic; Hank and Abby Hayes, who faithfully looked out after Tom and Taka in their perilous times; The George Wellhouser's, who ran the gas station and plumbing shop; The Bill Harding's who drove the Greyhound bus to Helena: The Crowley's, our farm neighbors; The Shannon's, our farm neighbors; The Fairweather's, our farm neighbors and many more, all of whom were loyal friends and neighbors that cared about the Oiye's during their trying WWII years.

CHAPTER 4

Montana State College

Why Montana State College?

C hoosing a college to attend is usually an easy choice when the student has certain skills and aspirations. To actually enroll there has many qualifications to meet. Good grades are fundamental to qualify at most private institutions and of course, the ability to pay the price is a major factor in determining where one actually enrolls. My choice of schools was the Montana School of Mines at Butte, Montana, ranked as the best mining school in the world, along with the Colorado School of Mines. Grades and aspirations were not a problem, but the affordability was not possible with only sixty-five dollars in the bank.

Montana State College was an A&M [Agriculture and Mechanics School] at near-by Bozeman, Montana. It was a land grant college where the tuition was fifty-five dollars for a three-quarter school year and was affordable. Jack and Bob Roadarmel and I registered in the engineering school. To conserve our assets we rented a basement apartment from Mrs. Potter, whose husband owned Potter's Drug Store on Main Street in Bozeman and we set-up housekeeping.

Except for the spin-dry washing machine that would require all three of us to hold it down during a drying cycle, everything was quite cozy for us country boys as long as our food didn't run out and we didn't gamble our chem-chips away.

After paying fifty-five dollars for tuition, ten dollars for our used books and lab fees, there wasn't anything left over for food, entertainment, rent and sundries, so we got some odd jobs and fortunately could bring a lot of food from home. My parents would send us lots of vegetables, fish and bakery things. The Roadarmel's sent us lots of wild game, cream, butter and fresh baked bread and eggs. We ate very well in the fall when we could hitch hike home and bring back seasonal things, but when the freezing cold weather started our diet got down to lots of Farina cooked with raisins and maybe a weenie or two. One quarter of that was enough and I got a room with Bruce Batchelder at Mrs. Germaine Alexander's' Boarding House.

The Yallerjanders

Mrs. Germaine Alexander [Mrs. A] was a unique and enterprising lady. She was of Belgian birth and married a very successful doctor in Big Timber, Montana. The *Yallerjanders* as they called themselves, had five children, Bill the oldest, Toinette [Toni] the second oldest was my age, James Cruthers [Jim], Douglas [Dooge] and John Randolph the youngest [Ranny]. Dr Alexander suddenly died after Ranny was born and Germaine was left to raise the family alone, except for her mother [Granny], who would come from Belgium as often as she could to help Mrs. A to cope with her lot in life.

Since she was a good cook, Mrs. A got jobs cooking for dude ranches and the boys and Toni worked on the ranches during the summer months to earn their way in life. They all waited on tables, cleaned up, helped with the horses and became expert horsemen. The love of dude ranching got into their blood. During the school year Mrs. A decided to start a local boardinghouse, but when Bill started college in Bozeman she decided to open one there and she leased a very large house near the college campus to provide lodging and meals for college students and teachers. This boarding house was known as the Brown House and was a hub of a lot of activities covering a broad range of students and teachers.

I was fortunate enough to be able to work for my room and board by tutoring the three younger boys, making beds, washing dishes, cleaning up the kitchen, shoveling snow from the side walks and doing any other odd job available. My mom faithfully put my freshly ironed shirts and pants in a denim covered cardboard suitcase and mailed them to me at the times that I couldn't make it home. During the other free time, I studied hard, played tennis, Toni challenged me with philosophical discussions, Bill played the piano for me, we all went to an occasional movie and had hot chocolate and popcorn afterwards and talked about owning a dude ranch some day.

ROTC

ROTC [Reserve Officers Training Corps] was a three-day a week requirement at all land grant colleges. All of the men had to wear US Army Infantry issued khaki colored woolens and polished brown shoes. We were issued Springfield 30.06 rifles fitted with bayonets and had to learn all of the army basic training manual of arms and care and maintenance of the weapons. Close order drill and parade marching with a band was required.

The army provided an organized rifle team of which I became the captain and our team won the 9th Corps Area championship.

4-C Enemy Alien

Pearl Harbor, was an unheard of place or word for most Americans, especially in Montana. On Sunday December 7[th,] 1941 it became a word that changed the whole world's way of life and thinking, alliances, military power and strategies, industrialization methods, ethics, spiritual values, world economics, control of the seas, division of land and territories, and it opened the doors to inter-marriages and unified trading of ideas and materiel. A black cloud fell upon the Oiye family.

On that day, one hundred and twenty thousand people of Japanese origin living in America became "Dirty Japs", an ethnic slur that cut one to the quick. By the stroke of President Roosevelt's pen, we also became "Enemy Aliens" without a country. No natural born Japanese male citizen was eligible for the draft, which I couldn't understand when we had not committed any crime against our country. Although my father had worked for the Cement factory in Trident for 17 years, in January of 1942 he was laid off from his job and fortunately had the farm to fall back on.

Jack and Bob Roadarmel and I were visiting their family friend's mattress factory in Bozeman, when the news came over the radio. We didn't have the foggiest notion as to what was happening and it took awhile for the reality to soak in. For me it was a solemn evening, even when Jack and Bob assured me of their loyalties as friends. My world really came crashing down after working so hard to be an American with Japanese hair and eyes. We all wondered about having to go to war and especially with Japan and all sorts of questions came to mind. The next day at school was a cautious one for me and I wasn't sure how to act, but when most of my loyal classmates and teachers, both men and women encouraged me that it wasn't my fault and our relationships even got better in some cases. Of course there were plenty of malicious bigots ready to make their presence known, but with my real friends the going was easier.

As soon as President Roosevelt declared war on Japan, all able-bodied men, 17 years old were required to register for the draft. When I registered, the hard part for me to try to understand was why I was given a classification of 4-C. I knew that 1-A was the most able and 4-F meant medically unfit, but, no one would tell me what 4-C meant. All that I knew was that all of my classmates and roommates were signing up for the Navy V-12 Program or for the Army Air Corps and I got rejected from both. Both programs allowed the student draftees to earn a college degree under a military grant.

Montana State College, MIT, Cal Tech and Michigan State were the four engineering colleges in the United States that were selected by the Army Air Corps to have an on-campus academy where student volunteers could earn a college degree while training for the Air Corps. Much to the chagrin of my friends, classmates, college deans, roommates, and myself, I was barred from enlisting in either program.

The irony of the situation was that, it was still a requirement for me to take ROTC and there were no restraints on me from becoming an excellent drillmaster and captain of the ROTC championship rifle team, both of which later became a detriment to my life in the all Japanese American Regimental Combat Team for having been a good college soldier.

The second year of college started out with literally a tough row to hoe because the college president shut the college down for two weeks while all male students went to the eastern part of the state to work in the sugar beet fields. I am told that Montana had the highest index of military volunteers, per capita by a factor of three, than any other state in the union and that Montana was very short on farm labor.

None of us had that kind of experience; although, the farmers treated us well and fed us well, we had a miserable time of survival. It rained ice-cold sleet almost every day and the fields were wet and muddy. We knew nothing about bending over, called stoop labor, picking up two or three pound sugar beets with a machete with a hook on the end, and then hacking off the green top and the root next to the bulb, without hooking or cutting your thighs or fingers.

The rows were about a mile long with a break in the middle. My roommate Bruce Batchelder and I were teamed with two other greenhorns and the shivering shaking, back-breaking work led us to find a way to cross the border into North Dakota, where we could buy booze. Montana was still a dry state. We bought several bottles of Canadian Club Bourbon whiskey and put a bottle at the ends and middle of each row so that we would have something to warm us up and to keep our backs straight. I had never drunk anything but home brewed brandy and choke cherry wine before this, so I got sick a few times. Good old Bruce helped me along. One would think that anyone with as much farming and hard labor that I was used to, I could have coped. I think that that experienced trained me for the Army. Oh Boy! Were we ever glad to get back to something as simple as schoolwork and a cold attic room?

During the second year of college, president Roosevelt devised, what he called the NYA, National Youth Recovery Act. This was a great thing for me because a lot of odd jobs came available at fifteen cents an hour. Janitorial work in the evenings isn't as bad as shoveling horse manure in the college barns. Oiling the machine shop tools and dressing belts was kind of fun because I got to learn how to use the machine shop tools and how to maintain them.

During the holidays, when the school shut down for maintenance I got to re-line our eighteen inch cupola with firebrick. That was quite a job because I had to squeeze into the cupola from the bottom and scrape the skin off of both shoulders to get the job done. I think that I was the only person small enough to get inside to do that job. Since my good friend Jerry Pesman, assistant department head was the teacher of machine shop and foundry; it was not difficult to get the job.

Mister Fred Homann and Jerry Pesman

Mister Fred Homann, Dean of Mechanical Engineering, needed an Engineering Librarian and he asked me to take the job. That was the best job that I had because I could go there and study and have all of the reference books and periodicals at my fingertips. Hardly any one came into the library and by that time Mr. Roosevelt had given us a raise to twenty-five cents an hour. I also became quite skilled on how to use and run a library and to maintain the stacks.

Mister Homann and Professor, Jerry Pesman, his assistant, were of German extraction and during WWI, they were both badly treated and had to struggle to get through school, so they had great empathy for my situation. In March of 1943, Mr. Homann went to the Adjutant General of the Army Air Corps Academy and fought to get me accepted into the Army Air Corps so that I could finish my schooling at the Academy. But he said, *"If you get five prominent reliable local citizens to write a letter of recommendation vouching for your loyalty as an American Citizen, I could then go to Butte, Montana and take a physical. If, I passed the physical I would be inducted into the Army Air Corps in about a week."*

My high school coach, Mr. Nobel Stevenson; store keeper, Mr. Lloyd Carver; store keeper, Mr. Joe McQuillan and; Dean of Mechanical Engineering, Mr. Fred Homann, all very kindly wrote letters for me. I went to Butte and passed the physical examination without a hitch. Naturally all of my friends and family were rejoicing that, George was going to be inducted into the Army Air Corps and all had a big party. I was given a lot of gifts, mostly Army air corps related. While I waited for my induction instructions, I went fishing and jumped for joy.

CHAPTER 5

WWII
[1943-1946]

Go for Broke

As we go through life it is never clear what our destiny will be or whom we will meet or be influenced by. The bubble not only burst on May 5, 1943, it disintegrated into the beginning of a nightmare of disbeliefs and anger at my country when I got my notice to report to Fort Douglas, Utah. I went from a [4-C] to a draftee into the Army Infantry and not the Army Air Corps, as promised and was denied obtaining my engineering degree.

The General had not only deceived me, but all of my family, classmates and friends because he surely must have known that Mr. Roosevelt had second thoughts about the 4-C classification of "Enemy Alien," so he rescinded the order and authorized the formation of an all Japanese American Regimental Combat Team of about 5000 soldiers in February of 1943.

Under secret orders, and in a blacked out troop train from Fort Douglas, I was shipped to Camp Shelby, Mississippi, to report to Colonel Pence, CO of the 442nd

Regimental Combat Team [442 RCT,] or better known as the [Go for Broke] regiment, *a Hawaiian gambling term for Shoot the Works.*

Getting to Camp Shelby alone in my one-size-fits-all wool khaki uniform it was 95 degrees Fahrenheit and muggy, which didn't help my newly acquired anger and disrespect for my country. In Montana it's cool and dry and two's a crowd, so to be dumped into the 442 RCT was probably the most shocking and discouraging thing that had ever happened to me prior to this day in history.

When I reported to the infantry my heart and mind screamed out "I n f a n t r y?" What happened to my promised Army Air Corp assignment at Montana State College? Thousands of shaved- headed Japanese looking little dark skinned men, that spoke in different tongues, all assembled in one place; who are they and why are they here? The military must be going to ship us to Japan or something? Why do they look at me funny and say strange things to me?

In Montana, that had only 600,000 people on 147,000 square miles of land and about 500 Japanese people scattered all along the railroad tracks and mines and farms, it was pretty frightening to be thrown into the 442 RCT crowd.

Rejection by Buddaheads

The moment that I joined the 442 RCT two-thirds of the recruits, about three thousand, who were 17-18 year old radicals from Hawaii, called Buddaheads took a dislike for me and did everything possible to pick a fight. It wasn't until forty years later that I found out that I epitomized a cultural difference between Mainland and Hawaiian born recruits. This paradigm of rejection made my life in the Army worse than actual combat and real bullets.

Coming from freezing cold Montana, at that time of

year my skin was bleached out and my nicknames became "Whitey" and "Montana," with a sneer in Pidgin English. ROTC, two years of engineering college, fourteen years of hard work, and expert marksmanship were detrimental credentials to own. However, also under attack and rejection were all mainland Kotonks, with whom I could communicate and who became my refuge and strength.

The PX or Post Exchange was the gathering place for off hours. Beer was available for enlisted men, which stimulated the Buddaheads, sitting on the floor on beer cases and engaged in boisterous gambling and to take on the Kotonks at every opportunity by blocking passageways and tripping them. If a fight ensued and the Buddaheads lost, then that night a whole gang would storm the tar-papered hutments and beat up on the singled out Kotonks.

Not a pretty sight and according to Senator Daniel Inouye from Hawaii, the 442 RCT was almost abandoned until someone encouraged them to take the Buddaheads to a nearby Japanese American Concentration Camp in Rohwer, Arkansas, where the families of many of the Kotonks were incarcerated. This sobering and unbelievable action changed the whole attitude of the Buddaheads and their paradigm went to zero and a new attitude arose to give the 442 RCT its heroic place in history.

My relationship with most of the Buddaheads got better and I made a few good friends, but it wasn't until many years after the war that all paradigms shifted and went to zero and those who hated me the most, now love me the most and are my very best friends.

Camp Shelby Mississippi

Camp Shelby meant a lot of firsts for me. I had never heard of a chigger, a macroscopic, six-legged, little red-mite that was small enough to bore into ones pores in a warm moist place like under your belt, under your collar, where your leggings or combat boots fit tight, the back of the knees and of course, the favorite place being the scrotum. All sorts of schemes were used to relieve the itching or to kill the little critters. Some resorted to burning them with a cigarette, putting gasoline on ones skin, putting DDT on them, pulling them out with tweezers, soaking in hot water, plain old scratching and, smothering them with fingernail polish. Those little buggers were worse than the enemy; at least you had an even chance with the enemy.

Walking guard duty around the camp at night, when the glowworms and lightning bugs were out, was a creepy crawly experience, especially just after a lecture or movie on enemy tactics. Loud snoring and grinding of teeth just as you walked passed an open shutter on the hutment, made the trigger finger on the rifle very nervous and jaw muscles very tense. Or to be challenged by the sergeant of the guards along some dark path in the woods, at night of course, left a few calling cards in ones drawers. I think I learned to be scared along with being a soldier.

Getting lost at night, on a patrol in the woods when the bats, owls, snakes, scorpions, tarantulas, roaches, and katydids are all turned on at the same time while a possum or raccoon hissed at you was not my idea of war.

A twenty-five mile forced march with full combat gear in eight hours in hot steaming Mississippi red dust is not an easy thing to forget when the standard stride is thirty-two inches and most of the Japanese American soldiers had to stretch a thirty-inch stride.

While sleeping one night I got beat up and hit on the head with a mess gear by the Buddaheads gang that was after another one of my buddies.

On the humorous side, on the rifle target range, I learned that "Maggie's Drawers" was a signal from the target bunker that the shot was a miss. There is a lot of speculation about the derivation of the idiom that won't be discussed. However, the signal was a red flag that was waved. The boys in the target bunker often played jokes on the battery commander or guys like me and gave us a lot of Maggie's Drawers.

Sus or Sazmo Ito

*O*nly by God's grace and mercy did I get assigned to Staff Sergeant Susumu [Sus} Ito's Detail Section of Battery "C" 522nd Field Artillery Battalion. "Sazmo", as Gus called him, became my lifelong friend, confidant and foxhole buddy.

Three years my senior, Sus was mainland born and raised and we shared similar interests. He enlisted in the Army in 1941 before Pearl Harbor and was trained at Fort Sill, Oklahoma to be part of the Cadre for the 442 Regimental Combat team. Bilingual, protective, gentle, low key, and intelligent are characteristics of Sus Ito that provided a bridge to fill the Japanese and Hawaiian cultural gaps, all of which helped me to adjust to the existing unfriendly and hostile environment between the Hawaiians [Buddaheads] and the mainland [Kotonks]. You will see a lot of Sus as our paths intertwined and his gifts of arbitration and mercy at work.

A Detail Section was comprised of a Section Leader, an Instrument Sergeant, an instrument corporal, two scout corporals, and a data recorder. After basic training I advanced to Instrument Corporal and on up to Section Chief, when Sus got a field commission. Our function was to be the Battery commander's right hand men in charge of knowing where, on a map, the battery was at all times, knowing what the gun coordinates were by survey, calculating all gun settings for a fire mission, keeping track of all firing data and results, accompanying Forward Observer Parties [FO's] to provide scouts and fire direction information for the

Commanding Officer, CO or the battery executive officer in charge of directing the guns.

An FO refers to a Forward Observer, who is usually a commissioned officer with a party of three enlisted men, a scout corporal, a radio operator or wireman and a battery carrier. This crew of four usually rode on a jeep or walked with the infantry troops. Sometime they rode into battle on tanks. To be chosen to be on the FO team from the battery personnel was a highly sought after position because most soldiers were eager to see the battle fought at the front line position at the risk of being a casualty. FO parties often times had to man an OP. An OP is military jargon for an Observation Post, which may be mobile or fixed depending on the nature of the front lines.

The mobile OP is usually comprised of an FO Party on a jeep or any other means of transportation that will put them as close to the battle-front or even behind the lines, circumstances permitting. More often than not, the FO party is assigned to accompany an infantry scouting patrol to gain target information and to direct fire on enemy targets. On the other hand, a fixed OP is usually one of long term defensive nature and protected by natural terrain features, bomb proof bunkers and long distances to targets, requiring high powered periscope type of binoculars and geodetically accurate reference points for precision fire control. An FO or a fire control sergeant and a communications person could man these Ops.

Sus Ito, Uke Minaga and I were assigned to ride with battery commander, Gus Ratcliffe, in his five-passenger command car to be with him at all times to provide him with radio communication with his battery convoy and headquarters. Sus and I provided him with position confirmation and fire control calculations. His driver was named Pvt. Herbert Uyeda, better known as "Pake", a Hawaiian Pidgin for Chinese because he looked Chinese. The five of us always made camp at some strategic place near the battery and got to be close friends.

As a bit of humor, Sus and I tied a tarantula up with a piece of thread and hung it on the doorway to Gus's pup tent so that it would jump his bald head when he got up. It was balmy warm day and there was no tactical activity going on so we had to wait a long time for Gus to wake up. Well, when he awoke, he crawled out of his tent and the tarantula did bite him on the head, he didn't even feel it. He just came out, yawned and made a cup of mojo [coffee.] I'm not sure what we were expecting, since we already knew that tarantula bites were not poisonous.

Yuki Uke Minaga

Uke Minaga, a genuine Kotonk was born and raised in Ogden, Utah so we got along very well. We had a portable chessboard that had little pegs for the men so that they wouldn't slide around while traveling. While we were hurrying up and waiting a lot, it became an ideal game for us to play. Uke got so good at it that the chess champion of France took him on in a match and just barely beat him. We even played by mail for many months after the war until our buddy Warren Tanaka disappeared and we found out that he passed away at an early age. Like Sus Ito, Uke is still a loyal friend. I will share more about him as we go along.

Louisiana Maneuvers followed basic training near Burr's Ferry, Texas on the Sabine River crossing at the northwestern border of Texas and Louisiana. The 442RCT was divided up into the Reds and the Blues. "C" Btry. was Blue. One of the first things that the boys wanted to do before getting started was to booze it up and bought a lot of tequila with a worm in the bottle and would see who could get the worm. Having not drunk anything since the college days, sugar beat episode, it wasn't long before old George was deathly sick. And when I woke up Sus and Uke had bedded me down in the command car and we were deep in the swamps somewhere before I was back to normal.

It was sometime in October when we got to Louisiana and it rained a lot, but we had a few good days of sunshine. Sleeping on the ground in our pup tent, Sus and I dug a trench around the pup tent to divert the water and collected long pine needles that were in abundance, for use as our bedding. Everything went fine until many domestic razor-back hogs, gone wild, came storming through our tent and uprooted us as well as leaving footprints up and down our anatomy. Every night we would have to re-set-up our tent and gather up our things that got scattered. On a rainy night it brought out a few choice names for those hogs. Some guys got so annoyed that they filled the garbage pit with slack lime and coaxed the pigs to eat it. By the sound of the squealing and grunting the antidote seemed to work.

Shepherd Bread

One of the big blessings that we still talk about is the big cloth bag filled with one-foot diameter flat-round hard loaves of shepherd bread that we were issued. This bread was so good toasted over a fire, or just as is in sandwiches, dunked in coffee and, believe it or not, used as foot rests in the back seat of the command car or even as a pillow. I think that the closest thing for comparison that we have today is San Francisco style sour dough bread with out the scored crust. Our bread crust was smooth and tough.

Many times the enemy bombed us with flour from an A-26 bomber or a B-25. When you got hit or sprayed with flour you were considered a casualty and the enemy got credit. To add insult to injury, if it was raining you got pretty gooey.

Lost in the Louisiana Swamps

One time Sus and I were supposed to conduct a survey-ing mission in the swamps while it was all clouded over and misty. Well we got lost for three days and got pretty hungry so we came upon an old farm shack and saw some chickens in the yard. We had heard about "Southern Fried Chicken" and our mouth began to water so we decided to knock on the door and ask for some food. An old looking lady, maybe fifty years old, came to the door and she and her husband with only a few teeth, welcomed us in and immediately poured us some coffee, which turned out to be pure chicory that was really strong and bitter.

We told the lady that we were hungry and would pay her to fix us some southern fried chicken. She agreed so in the mean time her husband kept saying isn't this coffee good. With tears in our eyes we would say yes and take a small sip. Some how the cups kept mysteriously filling up. We talked about the war and their travels. They were both born within a mile of their house and had been as far as Burr's Ferry, which was thirty miles away. After about two hours the lady came in with two scrawny drumsticks and two biscuits. We asked her where the rest of the chicken was and she said that she threw it away because she thought that the legs were all that you ate. It turned out that they never cooked a chicken before and had seen a picture of some one eating a drumstick. We couldn't cut, bite, or chew the chicken it was so old and tough. After we ate the biscuits we paid her and took the chicken with us in our pocket.

Being hungry enough to eat the bark off of a pine tree, we went down the road about a mile and came across a young boy, so we asked him if he would go home and ask his mom to make us some sandwiches. He looked scared and said, okay. About an hour later he cam back and gave us two sandwiches wrapped in a dirty old newspaper. After we paid him, he ran for home as fast as he could go. Our sandwiches turned out to be a cold, greasy lard cooked, potato on a slice of very gray looking bread with big holes. Boy! Was it ever good! Today, when we sit down at a New England clam and lobster bake at Dr. Sus Ito's beach house in Manomet, Massachusetts we reminisce about those meals in Louisiana.

Every day on maneuvers it seemed to get colder and colder and wetter, so by Christmas the rain was freezing on the long needles of the pitch pine trees where we were bivouacked. The trees bent over from the weight of the ice cycles and broke the limbs, which came crashing down like spears. I was told that some infantry guys actually got skewered.

One of the saving graces that took place was the fact that these pitch pine forests had stumps that were almost solid pitch and burned profusely even in the rain once you got them started. The only problem was that the fire spewed out billows of black smoke and it was long before everyone looked like they came from the south.

Up until now, I don't think I was ever that cold through and through, with every GI issued clothes on that I had in my duffle bag. When I got a furlough to go home in February to Montana, it felt so warm that I went around with my sleeves rolled up.

Government Rejects

While on furlough two new Japanese American, Government Rejects, came into my life. They were the husbands of Happy and May Koga, who came to Montana to live with Mr. and Mrs. Koga to escape the evacuation order. Frank Miwa was Happy's husband and Mike Miyake was May's husband. They both got whatever jobs they could, including, working for Tom Koga during the busy seasons. Frank later went to work chick-sexing school in Mankato, Minnesota and became a very prominent chick-sexer during the spring months. That sounds like a woman-izer, but he is one who determines the sex of a chicken the day that it hatches. After the war Frank and I worked together on several jobs and did a lot of fishing. Frank was probably the most nonchalant and forgetful person that I ever met.

Getting Ready to Ship Out

Overseas packaging of the detail section's instruments and equipment required maximum amount of prepara-tion and recording of packing lists. Every item had to have special preservatives applied and special overseas wrapping paper and cartons plus shipping boxes of certain sizes and weight. We spent two weeks making sure that all of our equipment was in A-1 condition and working, as well as being properly packed.

Sus and I had cameras, which we smuggled into the instrument boxes and were prepared to pay the penalty of being caught. There is no measure to describe the value that this breach of security has done for authenticating much of the 522 FABN's history. Sus took over 2500 actual combat photos, whereas my 1500 larger format photos were mostly portraits and non-tactical scenes.

Shipping Out

Upon arriving at the overseas staging area at Camp Patrick Henry, in New Port News, Virginia, we got a taste of what the magnitude of the army was, just at one port.

The logistics of just feeding this sea of men was unbe-lievable. We stood in line for breakfast from six o'clock to ten o'clock or so; and when we got fed we turned around

and stood in line for lunch and again for dinner. The serpentine lines must have been several miles long. The 442 RCT
was divided up into two shiploads on Kaiser built Liberty
ships. Our ship was the SS John Hopkins. I don't know who
John Hopkins was and why the ship bore his name.

After hours of waiting our turn came to climb the gangplank with full gear including a duffle bag. Aboard ship we
were herded into a mid-ship hold where our four tiered bunks
were. I got an upper bunk and had to climb up to get there and
had a few inches to spare from banging my head into the deck
flooring. Who ever the welder was that welded the seams on
that deck must have been fresh out of welding school on
his/her first job and to lie there and inspect those welds for
twenty eight days left me with white knuckles a time or two,
especially, when a couple of ash-cans were exploded very
near to our ship and caused it to shudder and shake. The fear
of drowning in an ocean bigger than anything in Montana
was not for me. I had never seen the ocean before and right
away didn't like the oily fishy sea smells and it's potential
power just waiting to take us to the bottom.

We got under way in the pitch black of the night. All
hatches were battened down and all merchant seamen were
in their places, when all of the sudden the ship rolled and
bucked a few times as we cleared the harbor and hit he open
seas. I was standing near the fantail when a seaman fell
overboard into the black sea, with only lights from the fluo-
rescing wake of the ship to see by. I hailed down a seaman
and told him that there was a man overboard and he told me
that, that was too bad because they couldn't stop for one
person. That was my first exposure to the seriousness of war
and a new way of thinking hardened my heart.

Every day was a different scene on the high seas and only
when the sun moon and stars were out did we have any feel
for what direction we were sailing at a maximum of five
knots per hour. It was an awesome sight to see ships of all

sizes and shapes from horizon to horizon all with their bows pointing in the same direction. I am told that there were over one hundred ships in the convoy. The signs that gave us some idea of what was going on was the fact that the weather changed from freezing cold to very hot within a few days and the ships that were on our left or port side were now on our right or starboard side, indicating that we were heading in the opposite direction from when we started. Sometimes we could here and feel an explosion near the horizon and smoke could be seen. Thank God, we were located pretty deep into the convoy and had a destroyer escort running along side except when they broke ranks to refuel and take on supplies.

Calisthenics and reviewing basic training aboard ship kept us somewhat in shape and gave us time on deck to breath in fresh air and to review the attitude of the ships around us. Of course a constant casino anywhere there was room on deck kept the boys happy. I was not a gambler since money came too hard to just throw it away

As we neared our destination we began to get buzzed by enemy aircraft so barrage balloons, which were gray colored rubber airship like balloons were flown from a long steel tether cables that were anchored to selective ships throughout the convoy. To my knowledge the balloons did a great job and we didn't loose any ships.

After about three weeks at sea the bread started to get pretty moldy and inedible. Penicillin was newly being made from bread mold, but in the raw form the mold was not useful. By this time powdered eggs were not the most savory breakfast foods either.

The Mediterranean Sea

Much to our delight and joy, one bright morning we sailed into the Mediterranean Sea at Gibraltar. What a beautiful sight that was to not only know our destination, but to see a sight familiar from our study of Geography in grammar school. Land looked so close that both shores could be easily seen. But, the Beautiful Mediterranean Sea was not blue. Africa and the Middle East had a huge plague of locusts and the water was yellow from the dead locusts. Every kind of fish imaginable was gorging themselves on those locusts and each other. Huge sawfish surfaced along side of our ship, sharks of all kinds were in the water bloodying up its color.

As we stood at the ships side rail, all of a sudden a huge black form came to the surface a few feet from our ship that turned out to be a British submarine. After picking ourselves off of the deck and seeing the British sailors and flag, we screamed and shouted our greetings and thanks.

That day we anchored off of Sicily where we could see Mount Etna smoking and the beautiful land. At this juncture the 442 RCT' s two ships parted company and we headed for Bari on the heal of Italy. The other ship landed at Brindisi, Italy a several miles south of Bari.

The Landing

Pulling into the harbor at Bari, Italy was quite an exciting and grim experience as our ship weaved in and out and around sunken ships in the harbor. We were all ready to disembark and were all lined up along the rail waiting for the skipper to dock the ship when he shouted orders to drop the anchor, which made a huge rattling noise and a big splash. Either the anchor chain was too short or the ship was going too fast because we crashed into the flimsy dock scattering anxiously waiting people in all directions. The impact was rather abrupt and some boys standing near the open gangplank area lost their duffle bags overboard and the rest of us behind the ships railing fell down.

It was a pitiful sight to see, for the first time, the grim ravages of war and real poverty. Here were our former enemies begging for food and trying to befriend us while up north the country was still at war with us. This created a lot of mixed emotions. Leaving the local Italian people in a lurch was our first hard order to carry out, as we trudged on to the train that was to take us across country to Naples.

Old French type, WWI forty and eight (forty men or eight horses) boxcars made up the train of three cars per battery. Our train was about ten cars long. It was so windy and cold riding on those dirty cars that we decided to burn the floorboards to keep warm and of course it was quite a sight to see, at night, as we lit up the countryside with all disregard for blackout regulations. It's a miracle that we didn't get strafed or bombed.

Welcome to Naples

Rum and Coca Cola, the most popular song in the states at the time, met us by the kids in Naples as we pulled into the station. The next thing that the sub-teen aged boys learned to do was to pimp for their sisters and moms in trade for cigarettes, chocolate, food or about twenty-five cents in lira. They didn't have any scruples about crowding in on the troops to make business, while their older brothers were up north waging war on us. We rendezvoused with the rest of the battalion near the town of Bagnoli, which was our staging area. Farther down the coast through a tunnel was the town of Pozzuoli, a fishing and tourist village, was where the locals were very friendly and some of the boys later married some of the girls.

Doon Toucha da Pesca

Four things that have stuck with me about Pozzuoli, were the fierce way the women would fight over a fresh catch of fish. I didn't realize that they would pull hair, claw at one another and even bite each other for a certain fish.

The second thing was the rate at which they could eat a big basket full of fresh clam-like shellfish, about the size of a little fingernail. While my buddy Shobo Doichi and I tried peeling those little mollusks to get the meat out of two or three of them, they had the whole basket eaten up. It was sort of like eating a gallon of salted sunflower seeds as fast as you can. While we sat there sucking on the shells the girls took off for greener pastures.

The third thing that impressed me was the baskets full of squirming baby octopuses that the fishermen brought in. They were sort of reddish brown and squirting black ink. The way the women snatched them up was no small sight to see. I always saw pictures of octopuses attacking ships, so I was amazed at the little size of the babies.

Number four, since the girls had taken off, we decided to try some spaghetti and got introduced to aldente-spaghetti. It was too hard for me to eat. Being wartime, the noodles were very dark, long and thick in diameter and the sauce was not very tasty. Much like "Southern Fried Chicken," "Italian Spaghetti," was not what we had in mind or read about. This was war; remember?

By this time, we had not unpacked our cameras, so we don't have any pictures of scenes in Pozzuoli. Some day I would like to visit the real Pozzuoli and just bask in the sun and stroll the beaches and eat some of those little shellfish.

Combat Staging

After unpacking all of our equipment and commissioning our new vehicles at the Bagnoli staging area, the 522 FABN joined the 442 RCT and embarked on and LST from Naples. On the dock at Naples with Mount Vesuvius in the background, we were able to spend a little time walking on the dock and talking to the people. The interesting and disillusioning thing was that toilets hung out over the sides of the dock and everything dropped into the sea. People with nets were catching shrimp and little fishes in the same water and eating them raw as they caught them. This was not a very delectable sight to watch as they sorted out the fishes from the excrement.

From Naples we steamed into Anzio and went on land via landing craft that went up on shore. Anzio had been taken as a beachhead several weeks earlier and a large ammunition dump was established there. The Germans were shelling the ammo dumps and occasionally the beach with their long-range eight-inch guns. One night they did hit one of the dumps and the fireworks was awesome to see.

On June 6, 1944 we got our marching orders and convoyed north toward Rome. Our command car arrived in Rome about 2:00 AM with the Victoria Emanuel white marble Monument gleaming in the full moon. There was a great deal of traffic confusion and poor road signs, so the route north to Civetavecchia, our destination was hard to find. Captain Gus being the leader that he was, somehow found the way and arrived at Civetavecchia at 5:00 AM, being the first battery of the battalion to arrive, instead of fourth as scheduled.

First Blood

On the twelfth of June, 1944 our battalion got its first baptism of fire and we were committed to the Rome-Arno Campaign.

The association of hot days, dry dust in the grape vine-yards and steep hills made one very thirsty and dirty and the stench of death, from bloated enemies covered with flies, never goes away from one's memory bank. I didn't have to go up to the front lines and spent my time manning the

Detail Section while Sus Ito and Uke Minaga went up front.

R&R

After two weeks of combat the battalion started sending four or five men per battery to Rome for R&R (Rest and Recreation) for a few days. I was one of the first from our battery to draw that duty and was really delighted to visit that beautiful and historic city. Like all tourists, the Coliseum, the St Peter's Cathedral and the Catacombs were awesome sights for a country boy from Montana to see and to try to project myself back that far in time.

San Martino Alla Palma

By the end of August we had reached the Arno River just south of Florence (Firenze) in a little town near Scandicci called San Martino Alla Palma situated high on a hill with a view of the Arno River Valley and a western corner of Florence.

Sus Ito and I set up an OP in a fancy Italian Chalet a few hundred feet below the Catholic Church that sat on top of the hill. Our job was to map out a zone of defense for the field artillery to zero in on, on both north and south sides of the Arno River and east and west as far as we could see. The purpose of the OP was to prepare it for turn over to the Brazilian Army, which was coming to relieve our command for the winter.

The Borgioli Family and Friends

While we were at this outpost, we scouted out the surrounding neighborhood and church and became very well acquainted with the local people. In a beautiful white marble two story house about 200 feet down the hill from our OP, lived a family of six; Mr. and Mrs. Borgioli; Marcella, twenty-four; Rensa, twenty-one; Marcello, eighteen; and Juliana, twelve years old. The family had a very large wine cellar under the stone house and many families from the neighborhood were hiding there at night when the Germans bombarded their village and courtyard.

Mr. Borgioli had a very bad case of gout from the coldness of the wine cellar and was in a great deal of pain, so being very cavalier I said "You should go back into your house and sleep in your own bed." He said "No! No! No! Tedeschi (Germans) bomb us." I said,"No, Tedeschi all gone."(Tutto Via)

After befriending the siblings, they were able to talk him into going back in the house. The first night was great but, the second night the Germans dropped a shell into the courtyard and old George's credibility went to zero and the Borgioli's went back into the wine cellar.

Mr. and Mrs. Borgioli were lovely people and unlike the people from the south of Italy they were very polished and proper. Even though Mrs. Borgioli was born and raised in Sicily, the home of the mafia type of people, she showed no signs of that culture. They had a restaurant in Florence, but the Germans had taken it over. Their house was all polished white marble inside. It was small but elegant. Bicycles were the mode of transportation and wine or vino was the standard beverage for everyone because the water was not good.

The Boy with a Hole in His Foot

Piero, a four-year-old neighbor boy was screaming his lungs out, so Sus and I went to find out what was the matter and found out that shrapnel from a German shell had hit him and it had pierced a hole in his foot. An older man named, Gusseppi, his grand father, was trying to treat the infected wound by pouring red wine in the hole and see sawing a piece of string through the hole to clean out the pus. We gave them some sulfa powder and Mercurochrome to put on the wound with some clean bandages. The wound started to heal in a few days and they were so grateful and hugged and kissed us and did a lot of arm waving like only an Italian can do. In December 1978 Mary and I went to visit him and I got drunk on wine at his house.

All of the siblings and neighborhood kids were anxious to learn English so we became good friends and we joined in with the neighborhood activities of making wine, harvesting and thrashing grain by hand and just sitting around and talking. We learned from Marcella and Rensa that they feared for our lives and wanted us to have some protection, so they invited us to attend the Catholic Mass the next Sunday and told us to meet them there, which we did.

We went into the church and sat down with them and of course all of the big eyes were on us and the kids were snickering. It didn't occur to us that we were surrounded by women. Much to our embarrassment, we discovered that traditionally, the men sit on the left side of the church and the women sat on the right side. That has always been a big laugh. On the way out the girls took us to one of the grottos or altars and prayed for us and lit a candle.

Afterwards they gave us a card with a picture of the Virgin Mary on it and Sus and I put the card in the top of our helmets and wore it the rest of the war as our guardian angel. When we finally had to leave, Renza, the blonde one, had become my good platonic friend, so she cried. I told her; after we won the war, I would be back. When Mary and I visited them we learned that Renza had died in childbirth and we met her son Renzo, who lived in Chicago.

Changing of the Guard

A Brazilian high-ranking officer and two staff soldiers arrived to take over our OP, right on schedule. Like the good hosts, Sus and I offered them a cup of coffee, which we boiled three times usual strength. Politely they took it and politely they spit it out because it was too weak. They told us that, in their country they like their coffee robust.

After spending all day training them where all the check point targets were, we had a pot of coffee Brazilian style. Shades of chicory from Louisiana passed in review as we parted company on that note and headed south to Vada, Italy and parted company with the Fifth Army and General Mark Clark.

Vada, Italy

Vada was a staging area south of Livorno near Cecina and north of Piombino on the Mediterranean Sea. While at Vada we were stationed on the beach and could go swimming in the ocean. For the boys from Hawaii and California, it was like heaven, but for me it was the first time that I had been in anything bigger that Yellowstone Lake in Montana.

Sus Ito, Toru Hirano, and Jim Mizuno lazily swam out a mile or so and I thought I could do that too, but it didn't take me long to get tired and I came very close to drowning.

Fishing with quarter pound blocks of TNT was the standard way of getting all kinds of Mediterranean fish that we roasted on the beach in seaweed. In the nearby town of Cecina, which was a fishing village we saw for the first time a very large Conger Eel and the local people made sure that we stayed away from their poisonous teeth.

While swimming in the Mediterranean Sea some of the

boys got badly stung by jellyfish and stingrays that were in abundance.

One Can Never Be Too Careful

One day the battalion was called together to learn how to disarm mines. Following the demonstration, the ordnance personnel loaded the ordnance items into a six-by-six truck. Just as they got into the truck something blew-up and the whole truck exploded killing six men. This was a grim way to be impressed by the safety precautions one had to observe when handling mines.

From Vada we were hauled by Merchant ships to Naples, enroute to France. Of real interest and coincidence, to me, was the fact that my friend, the famous Fly Fisherman, Bud Lilly from Manhattan, Montana was a seaman on the ship that hauled us. Bud and I grew up within ten miles of one another during the depression years and have become fast friends since.

Pompeii

Pompei, the evil city buried in the ashes of Mt. Vesuvius was a must-see before going to France so, without knowledge of it's history some of us got passes to visit the well preserved ruins of the ancient city. What an eye opener to be exposed to pornography at it's worst at the time. This naïve country hick had no idea that men and women lived that kind of a life style.

What caught my eye was that the marble door stoops were worn down several inches where men visited the brothels.

I don't seem to have any photographs or souvenirs from there, so I must have been too embarrassed or felt guilty about keeping them.

Beachhead in France

From Naples we were loaded onto Navy Transport ships. Such luxury we had never known since being in the Army. We had steak and potatoes every night, movies anytime we wanted to watch them, real pastries baked aboard ship, pancakes with bacon and real eggs, real coffee, fresh fruit, cigarettes and cigars and clean bunks. Thank God for little favors along the way. This however was not the smoothest ride that we had going around Corsica.

The beachhead landing, north of Marseilles and near Aix en Provence, France was anything but smooth. A huge storm had come up and the ship bobbed around like a cork while anchored about a mile off shore. Anyone on foot had to go over the side and climb down a large rope net and drop off into a landing craft (LCI) as it bobbed up and down along side the ship.

From the rail, I looked over and saw my buddies successfully making the drop, except for Fred Oshima, the oldest guy in our section. I saw the landing craft come up and over Fred as he was going down and was sure that he was crushed or scraped off of the rope ladder. But, by some miracle on the next wave he was still there and was able to make the next drop. My heart skipped many beats since Fred was very close and dear to me.

Upside Down

Next it was my turn to get my jeep into a larger landing craft for vehicles, so I got into my jeep, that had all of the instruments and some of our heavy gear. The crew put cable loops around both bumpers and hoisted me over the side. By this time, the ship was rocking very heavily and the wind and heavy rain had increased so much that my jeep started to bounce. Some how the cables slipped and the next thing that I knew was that the jeep had flipped over and I was hanging on to the bent steering wheel for dear life.

The crew took me back into the hold, turned the jeep over, straightened the steering wheel, checked the jeep to see if it would start, which it did, and gave it another try. This time we made it without a hitch and fortunately all of the instruments and gear landed in the landing craft on the first attempt.

Mud and Toilet Paper

Once on shore at the Septemes Staging Area, sergeant Ito's section was assembled and given a spot to pitch our tents. Mud over the tops of our shoes wouldn't hold the tent pegs, so we had to find rocks to hold the tent pegs down. The wind was so severe that almost everything went sailing across the countryside and all of the toilet paper seemed to stop on our tent ropes and poles.

This was not a comfortable place to be while we waited for a longshoreman's strike to end in Marseilles so that we could get food and supplies before moving north.

Hot Chestnuts

The wind and rain finally stopped and the sun came out long enough for us to clean up our gear and to get warm. We even got a pass to go in to Aix to visit and were shocked to see Frenchmen walking down the street with a girlfriend on their arm and urinating in the street gutters. In Aix they had beautiful chestnut trees and street vendors were roasting and selling hot chestnuts, which we bought and ate with great relish.

The Vosges Mountains

On about 30 September the battery made a 450 mile road march in France, north to Lyon and Dijon then northeast to a staging area near Fays, France in the rugged, heavily forested Vosges mountains of many small valleys and peaks.

We were assigned to General Dahlquist of the 36th, Texas Division of the Army. Heavy rain and snow began to fall and the gun emplacements became camouflaged-mud holes. On one occasion three of our trucks got mired down so badly that a Sherman tank tried to pull them out and got stuck almost up to the turret. A tank snatcher vehicle finally came to the rescue while a German Messerschmit made a few wild strafing passes over them.

We had to be very observant and careful when we got off of the normal path or into the woods because the booby traps and mines were everywhere. Taking care of physical needs became a carefully planned excursion into the woods to make sure that a trip wire wasn't stumbled over or you didn't hang your coat on one and set off a mine.

At night one could be assured that the bed check bombers and screaming mimmie rockets kept coming in bursts of six, to keep us on edge and with chills running up and down our spines from the rockets keeping one awake. This was psychologically demoralizing.

The Battle of Bruyeres

When our orders came to engage the enemy I was assigned to Lt. Chet Girard's FO party on a jeep with our mission to support "K" Company of the third infantry battalion in the capture and liberation of the town of Bruyeres, a main railroad and arterial highway junction between France and Germany. On one side of the narrow valley was the Vosges Mountains in France and the Black

Forest on the other side in Germany. The entrance to Bruyeres was heavily barricaded with large pilings and trees and boulders.

After three days of battling our way thru the mountains we came to an opening where we could see the road bock and the town of Bruyeres, so Chet's FO party fired on the blockade but didn't totally blow it up.

The 232nd Engineers came in with prima cord, which we saw for the first time, and wrapped it around all of the big timbers and in one shot, cut them all down so that the road could be cleared.

As we rode into Bruyeres there was much rejoicing and praising us for liberating them. But, what has never left my mind is seeing an older lady with a long handled, home-made stick broom, sweeping the street with great vigor as if to be taking her frustrations out on the war. This scene impressed me so much that I took a snapshot of her.

The Original Rambo

Having reached our objective, Chet went back to the battery and I was assigned to join O'Connor's Task Force, who's mission was to make sort of an end run around a little village named La Broquaine, a German stronghold, in the south end of the valley on the Bruyeres-Belmont Road. This required going through some very rugged mountain terrain at night. Al Binotti was like a Billy goat going through those mountains. He was a hard man to keep up with and I have always thought of him as the, " Original Rambo." He had four other men with him, whom I did not know. I do not know how or why I was chosen to accompany them on this task. When we reached an open spot, at daybreak, where we could get a good view of the houses that the Germans occupied, Al laid down a barrage of artillery fire that wiped out 80 grenadiers dead and 60 wounded plus several tanks and armament.

All men on the task force were awarded a presidential unit citation except for me because I was not listed as a participant. I did not know about this until after the war. Some day I would like to search the Army archives to see if my first sergeant or battery commander made that entry in their records.

The Lost Battalion Forward Observers

Upon arriving back at good ole' Charley Battery, cold wet, hungry and pooped, I was met by now Lt. Sus Ito, and Capt. "Gus" Ratcliffe and notified that I was selected to act as a forward observer for the "Lost Battalion," because there were no officers to take the job.

My FO party was made up of T/5 John Nishimura from New York City; Pvt. Eddie Ichiyama, from Honolulu, Hawaii; and PFC Richard Kurohara, form Hakalau, Hawaii. We were assigned to support Company "K".

Lt. Ito's crew consisted of T/4 Uke Minaga from Ogden, Utah; Sgt. Fred Oshima, from Richmond, California; and Sergeant George Thompson from Hilo, Hawaii. They were assigned to support "I" Company.

In the pitch black night, with a cold rain pouring down we were guided uphill into the forest toward "Banzai Hill," where the third battalion infantry troops were assigned to rescue the "Lost Battalion." It was so dark that we had to tie white handkerchiefs on the guy ahead of you and hang onto him so that we wouldn't get lost or separated. How we ever got to our destination will always remain a mystery to me.

To add to our fear and already shaky psyche, "Axis Sally" came on the loudspeaker and gave us the password.

Komrad, Komrad!

Fear and trembling set in when we reached the command post and reported in to the company commander. He said, "Start digging in the enemy is all around us." That required feeling around for a place to put one's rifle and backpack and to use the little folding trenching tool to start digging in the rocky soil without making any noise.

He was right! When I was scraping out a hole, a deep guttural sounding voice from behind me said, what sounded like "Komrad, Komrad." After hearing all kinds of horror stories of guys being garroted with a wire or silently bayoneted in the dark of the night, it really unnerved me as I groped around with outstretched hands to see what it was all about. Suddenly, I touched a person waving a white handkerchief and he again said "Komrad."

What to do, now? My gun was against a tree and my trenching tool was in my hole. I turned the German soldier around and headed in the direction of the command post making noise to arouse the guard. When, out of the dark came, "Halt! Password?" By this time I had forgotten the password and should have been shot. But by the Grace of God I convinced the guard, whom I could just barely see an outline of, that I was one of the FO boys and I had a prisoner. *Some nights I still jump out of bed when a strange voice is saying "Komrad."*

In the dim daylight we discovered that we were all on a very narrow ridge and that Ito's crew and mine were shoulder to shoulder. To my joy and comfort Lt. Sus Ito was right next to me, so we acted as one FO party of eight men until the two infantry companies split up. After we moved up the ridge a few yards the trees got very thick and the moss was knee deep in some places around the big boulders. In the moss was buried German mines called "Bouncing Betties," that were set off by trip wires buried in the moss. They would first jump up about six feet before bursting and scattering shrapnel of all kinds in all directions, while mortar shells, sniper bullets and tanks fired point blank into our midst's. Progress was very slow picking our way up the hill toward the lost battalion of Texans from the 141st Infantry regiment of the 36th Division. This hill became known as "Banzai Hill" when General Dahlquist ordered us to charge up the hill. It was here that his aide, Sinclair Lewis's son got killed.

The "**Click**" of a bayonet locking into place, sent chills up my spine as the soldiers charged up the hill. Sus's radio operator, Uke Minaga was awarded a Silver Star medal for making the first forward move up the hill and every one followed.

Whenever the company commander called for artillery support Sus and I reviewed our position, the best we could, and fired a round and listened for the burst. With a few calculated risks we fired another round and sometimes were quite successful.

By the time that we got to the top of the hill all troops were pinned down and casualties were running very high. I was asked to accompany an infantry patrol several hundred yards ahead of the main body to see if we could locate enemy targets that were giving us so much resistance and to see if we could pinpoint the "Lost Battalion." The enemy very cleverly disguised themselves and allowed this patrol to come behind their lines and come back out without a shot being fired. I was fortunate enough to be able to see some significant target check points in the valley between Biffontaine and La Houssiere and to determine the exact location of our guns by firing a few rounds.

When the patrol got back out and reported in to the battalion commander, it was decided that I-company would come around the hill to the right and K-company would go down the hill to the left, so Sus and I parted company. The minute that K-Company jumped off, we ran into the fiercest battle that we had ever seen. The German's had cleverly set us up and opened up with everything that they had and almost eliminated us before we rescued the 'Lost battalion."

To see officers in hysterics being chased down the hill by burp guns and snipers while General Dahlquist charged up the hill, with pistols blazing and yelling obscenities at the Germans and at us, his own troops was an unforgettable scene.

All of this action was being punctuated by mortar shells, tree bursts, dive bombers, rifle fire, mines exploding, rain and sleet, men screaming for help, the thud of a human flesh being hit by a bullet, trees being torn to sheds. I was personally blown thirty feet by a German 155 shell that totally deafened me and ruined my ears for life before we reached the Texans.

Sometimes it felt safe for me to just lie down on the ground and cover my head with my raincoat to shut out reality. What invariably happened when the battles were the thickest and the fiercest I had to go to the "benjo" (Japanese for the John), does that tell you something?

Uke Minaga, Sus's radio sergeant, recalls being one of the first to hand Buck Glover, whom we later met, a cigarette.

I don't remember of ever having made personal contact with individual Texans, which was anti climatic to what we had just survived.

Sergeant John Satake

S/Sgt John Satake K-Company, mess sergeant is a name not to be forgotten. He was the bravest cook that I know. John would personally bring hot meals at times to the troops on the line to keep them encouraged at the risk of his own life. If you recall, John was my old friend from Harlowtown,

Montana that I worked for on the railroad, when I was in high school. One day he came to me on the battlefield carrying a can of honey. He wanted to show me the label and how small the world is. The label read, *"Three Forks Headwaters Farm-Carl Feistner,"* my old friend and neighbor. How can it be?

After we celebrated the rescue of the "Lost Battalion," which has become one of, if not the most famous battles in American history, we thought that we had finished our job, but our orders were to continue on down the hill to secure all of the ground to the valley. By this time John Nishimura, Eddy Ichiyama, Richard Kurohara and I were four beat up and worn out GI's and couldn't wait to get on Kokomo's jeep, when he came to get us. I have no idea how Sus managed to take our picture being hauled out alive.

Days later we found out that K-Company had only eight riflemen left and I-Company had only four. We had over eight hundred casualties rescuing the two hundred twenty three Texans. Other numbers have been quoted depending on whose account you read.

The hot shower and rest that followed those twelve consecutive days of touch and go, for me, were like being in heaven with a whole new solemn lease on life and recurring flashbacks.

Champaign Campaign

Following the "Lost Battalion," effort. The 442 RCT was given the unique job of occupying the Riviera from Cannes to Menton, known as, "The Champaign Campaign." Some troops had a ball and several soldiers' married French women after the war. We were also assigned to policing and holding the Maginot line in the Maritime Alps between France and Italy, from Sospel to Menton, while regrouping and replacing our troops.

Sospel, France

On the 19th of November of 1944, C-Btry of the 522FABN was ordered to motor to Sospel, the farthest point north. To get to Sospel we had to pull our howitzers up a very steep, narrow winding road from Menton, through L'Escarene, at the bottom of the treacherous snake road of thirteen switch-backs in one place going up the side of the rugged bare-mountains. These switchbacks were so tight that we had to disconnect our howitzers several times and to push them around by hand, to negotiate the turns. Just that one place in the road that rose, several thousand feet took at least half a day to climb. It reminded me of trying to put a rattlesnake in a bag without getting bitten. Cannoneers and truckers were pretty well beat after that episode.

When we got to Sospel it started to snow and the Hawaiian boys were guaranteed their first white Christmas. Our job was to take over the French Maginot Line emplacements over looking the Bevera River into The Maritime Alps in Italy. There was a great abundance of Chestnuts from the trees at Sospel and we ate them raw, boiled, roasted and mashed. Everyone that wanted to got a chance to man the OP that we had there that winter. Although it was cold and wet we got a chance to build fires, do our laundry and get cleaned up in general.

In January 1945, C-Btry was moved to Menton and assigned houses to stay in and to maintain the OP's on the French-Italian border. FO parties consisting of an officer or Chief of Detail and anyone who would wanted to go up the side of the mountain, by mule train, from sea level to about fourteen thousand feet in sub zero weather, could man the OP's for a week. This was pretty good duty although quite hazardous. Several times the trails were so narrow, slippery and close to the canyon wall, that even the sure footed mules would bump their packs on the mountain and fall straight down into the ravine. Everything would be lost.

Only kindness and gentleness, in spite of what the stories are about hitting a mule over the head to get its attention, will get an Army mule to work for you. An experienced mule certainly knows a lot more than a field artillery person about packing, geodetics and trailing. When the trail got too steep to keep up with the mule, we used to grab his tail and get towed up the hill. The only problem with that was that it would bray a lot from the rear and one had to learn to breathe between outburst. The other thing bad about the mules was that they brayed at night, giving away our OP position.

Since this was a rather non-tactical location, the Infantry boys would string wire all along the steep hillsides and tie tin cans to them so that at night any enemy infiltration could be detected. We had quite a few alerts, which turned out to be animals or rockslides, at least on my watch.

One good thing about this duty was that it gave us a lot of practice sharpening up our shooting skills with other field artillery pieces able to reach distant targets.

Gotcha!

My pride and joy and reward for manning one OP, that overlooked the Italian coastline and the Mediterranean Sea, was that one bright sunny day, I saw two Navy Cruisers in the bay about twenty miles out and simultaneously spotted a huge railroad mounted 320mm, German long tom being pulled out of a tunnel, at least twenty miles up the Italian coast.

This gun had been firing a couple of harassing rounds a day toward Nice and could not be located because the coast was usually foggy. But on this clear day it was easy to see the smoke ring and identify the round as it went on its way to Nice. I pinpointed the location on a map and radioed the coordinates to DIVARTY (Division Artillery) and requested fire from the two cruisers. One moving ship immediately fired one round within a hundred yards of the target. I gave them a sensing and called for "Fire for Affect." What a beautiful sight to see the gun go tumbling into the sea as those Navy eight inchers fired a full broadside while on the move. To this day, it still gives me goose bumps to recall that scene. Here again only a couple people believe this story because it was, to my knowledge, never publicized.

Menton, France

Menton is a beautiful French Resort town right at the Italian border, where the Italian Riviera begins with a railroad track running between the two countries.

The architecture was very massive Mediterranean style with palm trees and Aloe type cacti in abundance. Citrus groves were everywhere on the rocky hillsides where the homes are nestled. Having a house to live in for the first time in a year was really luxurious, but not good for my health.

The first thing that happened to me was that I got the flu that turned into bronchitis in spite of all of the new, huge sulfa tablets that the aid station gave me. The pills did nothing but to cause the skin to peel on my feet. I was sent to the hospital in Cannes for two weeks, where I had a tonsillectomy and was quite miserable trying to swallow and shivering from the cold.

On getting back to my unit, my buddy, Uke Minaga and I decided to explore and loot some houses near us. We didn't find anything that we wanted, but we got covered with fleas that literally ate us up for our punishment. The only way we were able to get rid of those little devils was to fill our sleeping bags with DDT and get in them with clothes and all. It's a wonder that we didn't get some kind of DDT poisoning. There is nothing like having a few fleas eating and breeding in ones jeans. I don't know which is worse chiggers or fleas? I think chiggers. No more looting after that.

One time I got a pass to visit Monte Carlo with Warren Tanaka and Mac Nishimoto. It was an awesome place and some of the poker chips were made from woven pure gold and silver wire. We all managed to get some of those beautiful filigreed chips for souvenirs, but mine were stolen in short order.

Germany and the Seigfried Line

On March 9, 1945, the 522FABN received its march orders to split off our superior field artillery unit from the 442RCT and join sub units of the Seventh and Third Armies, in Germany to help breach the Siegfried Line. On an overcast night, near Saarbrucken, at the town of Klein Blittersdorf we crossed over into German soil. Artificial moonlight was provided by the signal Corps by bouncing many huge anti aircraft searchlights off of the cloud cover. This provided just enough light to help us walk through a minefield. I was deeply impressed by this ingenious use of the elements at hand.

I was attached to an unknown infantry outfit and as we walked into the mine field one of the foot soldiers walking in front of me stepped on a shoe mine that blew his foot off except for the Achilles tendon that his foot hung by. We both fell down and the big six-foot blonde soldier was telling me to shoot him because the pain was so bad and he thought that he had lost his private parts. When I finally convinced him that he was okay, I tried to carry him out of the minefield, but the dangling foot kept getting tangled up so he said cut it off which I did and finally got him to a medic. This was a bit unnerving and unbelievable for a field artilleryman to do this and an awful welcoming to German soil. I have often wondered if that soldier's foot could have been saved if it hadn't been cut off.

From this point on I was assigned to various FO Parties depending on the officer who needed my skills. The legendary Siegfried line turned out to be a piece of cake and we met very little resistance until we got to Worms on the Rhine River. Near Worms I saw a deer running through the woods, which was an easy shot for a Montanan. The heck with the war, fresh food was a better choice.

A Dud

While in a fruit orchard near Worms, Germany Sus Ito and I were on reconnaissance when we got spotted and were shot at. We jumped into a dry irrigation ditch and we watched a big slow moving 155mm howitzer shell coming through the trees toward our jeep. It was hard to believe that that shell bounced off of the hood of the jeep and never exploded. You have never seen two happier guys for being spared again. Our thoughts were that our good luck card in our helmets was hard at work watching over us. When the dust cleared away our good old jeep sure kicked up a lot of its own dust racing down those rows of trees and into better defilade. I don't think we recommended that we put the battery in that area.

At Worms the Infantry group that we were attached to had made a pontoon bridge on the Neckar River where it joined the Rhine River at Lampertheim, north of Mannheim-Heidelburg. Some of the other bridges were being heavily strafed and bombed in the distance from where we were. From that point on, the war became a foot race toward Munich, the SS Headquarters. We crossed the Tauber River near Rothenburg and headed south to Ulm where we crossed the Danube River.

In Bavaria there are many rivers that drain the southern side of Swiss Alps and the Austrian Alps that all drain into the Danube and Rhine Rivers so we were constantly crossing a river on our southeast course through Bavaria.

At Ulm, Germany the only thing left standing, from Allied precision bombing was a very tall church building, which to me was an unbelievable sight. The other thing that impressed me was the fact that the beautiful blue Danube River was anything but blue.

Before reaching Ulm when we got into the mountains near Aalen we encountered some factories making aircraft parts. Plywood painted like green trees surrounded these factories, for camouflage. The workmen, not knowing who we were, busily kept right on working as shown in a photograph that I took. We later learned that this was a kommando, where slave labor DP's (displaced persons) worked and were afraid of the Gestapo.

From Ulm we crossed the Lech River near Mertingen and Augsberg, where we captured an Airfield. German aircraft were designed and tested here. This place was a real prize for a mechanical/aeronautical engineer to get many reels of 35mm movie film showing Adolf Hitler and Hermann Von Goering watching the experiments blow up on the runway and in flight.

Cheese and Sardines

Someplace around this area we came across a food supply depot that had big rolls, the size of an automobile tire, of cheddar cheese and cases of Portuguese sardines. It was quite a sight to see everyone rolling cheese and carrying sardines down the road. Needless to say, we got constipated and our skin started to get shiny from the sardines. That was like turning a kid loose in a candy store.

War was secondary for a few days.

One highlight of my career in Germany was when one of three 522FABN scouting parties, of four men each, captured eighteen Germans. The party that I was in, consisted of Capt Gus Ratcliff, T-4 Uke Minaga, Toro Hirano and me. We spread out and Capt Gus and I saw some Germans in a hunting lodge, so we sneaked up on the house and started shooting and by the time Uke Minaga and Toru Hirano arrived to get in on the shooting we had captured seventeen prisoners and I shot one in the leg that was making a run for it. LT Sus Ito and Sgt Fred Oshima captured three more while Pfc Norimasa Yamahiro and Pfc Yoshiacki Kobatake captured two making our total bag of twenty-three for the day.

Of interest was that, when Capt. Gus reached the house I saw him run face to face into a German guard who threw down his gun and put his arms up. In his excitement Gus pulled his bolt back on his carbine and the clip fell out on the ground. Fortunately, he was behind the guard and recovered the clip and kept command of the situation.

The Main Dachau Concentration Camp

Dachau was an infamous main concentration camp in Germany that was operated by the elite SS troops, located six kilometers north-west of Munich. It was not a military target for the 522FABN and was not in our battalion's line of march.

Because the forward observer and G-2 parties were mobile and sometimes as much as twenty miles ahead of the infantry we didn't stay exactly on the battalions designated course. The road conditions and military activities pretty much directed our paths, thus some of the Japanese Americans actually entered the crematoria at the main camp at Dachau on 29 April 1945 in heavy rain and assisted the

45th and 42nd Divisions of the Seventh Army in the liberation of Dachau' s main camp.

Surrounding the main headquarters camp at Dachau were over one hundred sub camps called *"Kommandos."* These Kommandos were spread out over a radius of about thirty miles from the main camp. They were comprised of various slave labor functions such as machine shops, vegetable gardens, clothing factories, medical research billets, armament factories, and etc.

How does one reconcile the fact that many of the mainland field artillery soldiers had families still in concentration camps in America and were now involved in liberating a Nazi concentration camp in Germany? Ironies of ironies, mysteries of mysteries, and miracles of miracles it became a reality and a bright spot in our colorful history.

The night of the 29 April 1945 it began to snow and the heavy wet snow covered everything to a depth of one foot or more in some places and lasted several days.

On May first, Sus Ito's FO Party of Uke Minaga, Tee Sugita and I were on the road near Dachau when we saw hundreds of lumps in the snow that turned out to be human bodies and skeletons. Having witnessed all those corpses that had been totally dishonored, starved to death, full of disease, over-exposed to freezing, or from pure exhaustion, and with disregard for human dignity left me with delayed emotional reactions of bewilderment, disbelief, disgust, remorse, anger, frustration, fear and hatred for the Nazi. *Most of all I felt guilt for the transgression of mankind to do evil in the sight of God. Any form of Holocaust is an ugly sight to be exposed to and carries with it the stench of death and evil.*

For the next two days we captured hordes of German soldiers and liberated several Kommandos with DP's in striped clothing inadequate for the clime. Some of the Displaced Persons (DP's) were on the edge of starvation and exhaustion while other younger men were robust and healthy, depending on what they were doing at the time. On our trail south we went through Starnberg, Bad Tolz, Waakirchen and ended up at Shaftlach on May the eighth, VE-Day.

The 522FABN had been attached to seventeen different units of the Seventh and Third Armies and its trucks were used to haul the 101 Airborne troops into Hitler's strong hold at Bertchesgaden when the War in Europe finally ended and the cold war with Russia started to take root.

The War in Europe Ends and Occupation Begins

At Shaftlach I was assigned to take over the town as a Burgameister and enlisted a young polish lady named Elizabeth, who spoke very good English, to act as interpreter. Our job was to sort out the DP's and get them into ethnic groups that could be all shipped to their native countries. Needless to say there was a lot of confusion and lack of orderly control.

Captain Gus was able to enlist a Lithuanian teenager named Larry Lubetski, whom we still keep in touch with in Mexico City. Larry stayed with our battery until Capt. Gus left Germany.

From the Waakirchen area, the 522 FABN was ordered to go northwest to occupy a town on the Danube River called Donauworth, a semi-walled in city. This city was pretty much flattened by allied precision bombing. Here again, two of the few buildings left standing were the five hundred year old church on the edge of the Danube River, this church was more Gothic in architecture and did not have a tall steeple like the other one that withstood the bombings. Under the first church was a tunnel that housed a large machine shop that overlooked the Danube River and railroads. The allied troops were careful about bombing churches and the Germans took advantage of the rules of warfare.

Fortunately, C-BTRY was given a very large elegant old bank building to occupy and we all had good sleeping quarters with a large kitchen and toilets. Our job was to establish a checkpoint on the road and sort out DP's and POW's and to load them into trucks or onto railroad cars heading to their homelands. Hundreds of both groups came by every day.

Another job that C-BTRY had was to police a DP Camp that was erected near Donauworth. This was a difficult job because the young DP men were angry with the Germans and were finding ways to murder them. One night when I was on patrol I heard a terrible blood curdling scream coming from a near by farmhouse. When my patrol got there, a woman had been raped and shot with a pistol made from an eight mm, bolt action Mauser rifle that had its barrel and stock sawed off. Not able to capture any of the villains made our job rather futile.

A long-term assignment was for me to keep the battery supplied with German servants to do the housework, help in the kitchen and keep the yard and grounds picked up. This required going to see the Burgameister at the Gast Haus or town hall every week to collect their pay because Germany was paying off their war reparations this way. The pay was a real joke at a measly two hundred and eighty-five pfennigs a week per person. Some times, I felt so embarrassed for them that I gave each a little more from my own pocket.

Being close to Augsberg, where good beer was made, our battery always had a twenty-five gallon rubberized canvas lister bag with four spigots full of German beer hanging in the patio of our quarters where one could fill a canteen cup anytime of day or night. That was good stuff but when it's free and so available we didn't drink too much. When VJ-Day came in August, the boys managed to make what they called "Atomic Punch," that was too potent for me and many others got smashed on it.

In September 1945 our Battalion began being sent home, by the point system. We were all given service longevity credits and numbered accordingly. Those with sixty-four points or less were shipped out to a quartermaster corps near Frankfurt, Germany where they were assembled. A week and a half later, we got orders to return to the battery in Donauworth and the resident battery personnel got disseminated throughout Germany and France and shipped home.

Charley Battery 522 FABN Splits Up

Being the ranking non-com from the original battery "C", I was put in charge of the battery as an acting first sergeant to bring the battery home without officers. True to form, the story of my life has always been second in command without the pay or the title. Although we had a contingency of sixty-four point first sergeants, master sergeants and mostly high-ranking non-coms, they were all treated like privates and had to do KP and guard duty.

Shortpants Hirashima was my mess sergeant; he was the shortest guy in the battery and had been a mechanic. He rode on racecars in the Indianapolis 500 with Mauri Rose and the Offenhausers. Sgt. Fred Oshima was assigned to be the battery clerk and helped me with the administration duties.

We had to make the boxes and crate-up all of the military equipment except trucks and howitzers. Closing down the facility in Donauworth became quite a job even to disposing of books and stuff left behind by the others was a chore.

After Shortpants had fed us a fantastic Thanksgiving dinner, we departed from Donauworth by train in boxcars to various staging areas along the way until we arrived at Le Havre, France. There we embarked on the SS Sheepshead Bay, on December 17, 1945, a Victory type ship, headed for New York City. The forty to fifty feet angry seas were extremely rough and the ships screws came out of the water many times while the ship wallowed and shuddered from the vibration all the way from the Azores to New York, making our progress very slow.

Two days before Christmas the storm got so severe that a spare forty-ton anchor broke loose from it's mooring s on deck and tore a hole in the railing as it went overboard. The captain came on the loud speaker said that the radar mast had been broken off, but not to worry, we would make it.

With everyone sick hardly anyone ate Christmas dinner. I remember going into the refrigerator to lie down and ate a lot of apples that seemed to stay down. Not much dispelled the fear of drowning after having survived so many near misses in the war.

In spite of the storm, when it was calm enough, the boys found time to gamble and some guy that never gambled before won most of the money.

New Years Day 1946

New Years Day 1946 our ship pulled into New York Harbor in a blinding blizzard. As the beautiful Statue of Liberty came dimly into view all kinds of paper money went sailing on by in the wind. The guy that had won all of the money gambling went berserk and threw it to the winds. She still looked almost sacred as we steamed on by to a five-hankie pass in review. America you never looked so good and it was worth it all.

From New York we sailed to Camp Kilmer, New Jersey where I had the privilege of signing over Charlie Battery to the Adjutant General on duty before they shipped me to

Camp McCoy Wisconsin to be discharged on January 4, 1946. The reason that I chose Camp McCoy Wisconsin was because my sister Peggy was living in Chicago and it was the nearest discharge place.

Chicago was a new beginning, but not without it's ironies and surprises. First of all who should be living in the apartment next door to my sister than my old buddy Uke Minaga, who had come home two months earlier. He had become good friends with my sister and her husband but had no idea that she was my sister, so we were both happily surprised. It's strange how things work out.

Secondly and ironically, it was a shock to me to find out that my brother-in-law Roy Ito had gotten a job as a tool and die maker in a factory making gun parts after he got out of Manzanar Concentration Camp in California. The carbine clip making machine that he was working on had the same code letters "MN" as the one that fell out of Captain Gus's carbine when we captured the eighteen Germans and he almost got shot by the guard that he encountered. How can it be that these things happen to me? A year later I went back to Chicago and helped Roy and Peggy and my two nephews drive to Montana before they went back to California.

On the way home from Chicago, I stopped in Cleveland, Ohio to visit my friend Professor Jerry Pesman, who had gone to work for NACA (National Aircraft Control Administration) showed me the first super-sonic wind tunnel built that took all of the power that the city of Cleveland had to run it. The airport was shut down for light aircraft because of the wind that it produced. He also showed me the advanced fire prevention measures for aircraft experiments that he was working on. When NACA became NASA (National Aerospace Administration) Jerry went to work for them in Houston and developed Biomedical hardware systems. He died at the age of ninety-one in Y2001.

Sus Ito located in Cleveland, Ohio so we had a good reunion before facing the real world.

Day of Remembrance

To close out this session on the WWII, I will note here that on February the 19th of Y2002, CH 54 (KTEH) of San Jose, CA featured the sixtieth anniversary of President Roosevelt rescinding the classification of **4-C** (enemy alien unavailable for military service). He authorized the formation of the famous 442nd Regimental Combat Team. I was graciously chosen to represent the 522nd Field Artillery Battalion in this feature story, which coincidently was on my eightieth birthday.

CHAPTER 6

Rows to Hoe

Welcome Home

Getting back to our farm in Logan, Montana was like being in heaven until reality set in. The war wasn't over! I learned from my parents that only their loyal local merchants and friends bought vegetables from them. My new friends Mike Miyake and Frank Miwa informed me that Japs were still Government Rejects and there was no local work for Japs except on Pop Koga's extra gang and on the section where Gabe Wada was employed.

One would think that fishing would be my first activity, but it wasn't. And no, it wasn't females either. I saw in the newspaper where someone wanted to sell a 1936 Chevy turtleback coupe for six hundred dollars and I just happened to have six fresh one hundred dollar bills burning a hole in my pocket. That was a hundred dollars more than they paid for it new twelve years ago but cars of any kind were as scarce as hens teeth and it was in mint condition. I was so proud of that car that my smile would not start hurting.

After Frank Miwa got back from his chick sexing season in Minnesota, he and I decided to go to work for

Mr. Ogata in Helena on his now, one-section (640 acres,) of land ten miles north of town. We were given the job of selling vegetables on a state wide scale, using his new one and a half ton Chevy van with a sixteen speed split transmission and air booster brakes for hauling.

On our first trip to Great Falls, I was driving and hadn't gotten used to shifting all of those gears, so the sixty-mile uphill trip through the mountains was rather hair raising at times. When we got to Great Falls we had to go down a narrow alley with a number of hotels lining both sides. The hotels had the old fashioned style of fire escapes hanging down in the alley and while I was trying to locate the Safeway store there was a scraping noise on our van roof and a huge noise as the fire escape from a hotel came crashing down. That made us two Japs even less popular.

Traveling south from Great Falls to Helena was down hill and down-shifting, to conserve the brakes, was essential, especially when we had a load of fruit aboard that we were hauling on the return trip. Things went fairly well until we got to the last turn before going down the long grade into Helena. We were going about fifty-five miles per hour on the narrow road and as I down shifted my foot slipped off the clutch and my knee hit the ignition switch and shut the engine off causing the air booster brakes to shut down as well. By the time we got to the last turn we were going seventy-five miles an hour. I was jamming the brake pedal as hard as I could with little or no effect. By the skin of our teeth we just barely squealed around that last turn and on to the straightaway. It took several miles before I could get the engine started again and to slow down enough to make the turn into the ranch.

Post War Rejection

Then came the trip to Bozeman and Livingston with a full load of produce to sell. It was dark when we headed out and before we got to Three Forks, Frank needed to make a pit stop, so I pulled over and when he got out of the truck he fell down the steep shoulder and got all battered. Fortunately his wife, Happy, in Three Forks patched him all up.

In Bozeman I went to all of the large produce distributors that were pre-war customers and they wouldn't buy from me. Rather than risk a trip to Livingston, which was another forty-five miles down the road I decided to call Mr. Ogata to find out if we should go on. In doing so, we went into a drug store, where they knew me from my college days, to make the phone call. The lady said I'm sorry you will have to go to the telephone office. I said "That's fine, thank you very much," and we drove to the telephone office. I called Mr. Ogata and he said, " It's your choice." My choice was to risk it.

When I came out of the telephone office there were three police cars with Frank showing them what we had on board. The head officer told me that we had to go to the police station for questioning while they traced my phone call. It turned out that the lady at the drug store called them and said that I was not to be trusted. After being detained for two hours, I called up my friend Fred Homann, dean of Mechanical Engineering and he came down and gave them the good word. By this time it was too late in the day to make the trip to Livingston and our load was wilting so we drove to the dump and unloaded it except for the potatoes. This was a big loss for Mr. Ogata but he kept us on making the Great Falls run.

That fall Frank and Happy moved to St Paul Minnesota. I decided not to go back to school yet and went out there to live with them in the spring while I got over being rejected for fighting a war.

When not working for Seeger Sunbeam Refrigerator Company making four name brands of refrigerator coils off of the same production line, we fished the lakes a lot for walleyed pike. Our good paying piecework job pooped out when I invented a way of doubling our production rate and the company management made that the basic production rate for piecework. We quit and I went back home to build a four-car garage for my parents for housing the farm machinery and two cars. I did this all by myself in four weeks. It was no thing of beauty but very functional and strong, being made from rough sawn lumber.

The Whisk Broom

The fall of 1946, I decided to go back to school and moved in with my sister Anita, who had gotten a job at the college during the war and worked in the administration building. She had a nice basement apartment at the Silverthorne's home in Bozeman, just two blocks from the Engineering Building. Jewel Silverthorne made the best banana cream pie that I had ever eaten and I would drive many miles for a slice of it. She was a very special lady and treated us all like family.

Anita was the best natured and loving person that I've ever known and would giggle at the drop of a pin. Her co-worker and best friend named "Tiny," was rather large and had the same sense of humor that she did. One cold wintry day when they were driving my father's Model-A Ford, they pulled into a service station and asked the nice young man if they had a restroom? He politely said, *"Oh don't worry about it ladies; if you'll just back it up over here, I will blow it out with air."* He thought that they said *"Whisk Broom."* You can just imagine the rolling in the aisles type of laughter that came out of those two. For years to come that was a standing joke around the campus.

Giants in my Life

Getting started in college again, after being out for four years, was rather strange and difficult. However, my old schoolmate, Bill Davis was right there to help me out. Even during the occupation of Germany, Bill somehow found me and we had a great reunion. He was also responsible for getting me elected to student branch president of the ASME (American Society of Mechanical Engineers.) I still make contact with Bill when I go fishing and pass through Bozeman.

Bill's dad, "Doc" Davis was in charge of the steam plant at the college and was always a loyal supporter of the Oiye family during our tough years. During some of those cold Montana winters, when the radiators froze up on campus, Doc Davis worked day and night to keep the steam plant running at its maximum output and Bill would be there helping. Now when I drive by that smoke stack I think about Doc and Bill Davis and their faithfulness.

Driving past the College Field House on campus reminds me of Charles Silverthorne relating how he was in charge of building the unsupported roof structure that fell in when it was almost completed. He told me of how difficult it was for him to be head of the manual arts department at Bozeman high school and having to face the disaster without giving up and *"going on."* When I think about that story, it reminds me of my life story and how many times I've been in charge and the roof fell in. *"I wonder who is really in charge."*

These giants left a few big footprints that taught me a few lasting principals of life.

Just Glen

Another significant classmate was Glen, his last name I've forgotten, but Glen I remember. Every chance that we got we would play tennis, study together, or spend time in the Student Union lounge comparing WWII notes. I guess one of the reasons that we got on so well was because we were of the exact same build, short, small, wiry, and both engineers with big engines. Glen made some skid marks on my blackboard of life that are there to stay.

One Sunday we set out to play tennis, while the weather was still good, but for some strange reason we simultaneously said, "maybe we ought to go to church." The question was, where? We got in my car and drove around town until we saw a little unpretentious looking little cottage like building that was called "The Church of Christ," in Bozeman.

My sister, Anita was one of those "Born Again" Christians and had talked to our family about becoming believers, but that was too "Religious," for me. Glen and I went into the church and the people were really nice to us. The no pressure preacher talked about some issues that recalled a lot of wartime miracles and instances that seemed to go together with what he was preaching. Every Sunday, in this little church they had what they called an alter call and without any pressure or coaxing people went forward and gave their lives to Christ as their Savior. Without hesitation Glen and I went forward and accepted Christ as our Savior. We then got in the car and drove off to the tennis courts and tore into one another without any discussion. So that ended our church going and I didn't tell Anita or anyone else about it.

My Nervous Breakdown

When winter set in Glen and I no longer played tennis and the basement apartment was very quiet. My ringing ears seemed to get louder and louder every day and one ear rang at a different frequency than the other, that actually made the situation worse. At night, flashbacks of the war became more frequent and studying virtually stopped. I would wake up struggling to avoid being bayoneted or hear the shells bursting in my room and my buddies screaming for help. One day after a terrible night, I had a nervous breakdown and had to quit school at the end of the second quarter, with all incomplete grades.

From that day on my whole life collapsed and started over. No one understood why I acted so strange. Mr. Koga and John Satake were kind enough to give me a job on the railroad extra gang as a timekeeper with my own little speeder to go down the tracks. I only had to keep track of the amount of work that was accomplished everyday and the amount of materials that was used plus handle the payroll for the hundred-man crew. This job was easy and gave me a lot of free time to go fishing and hunting in some of the most remote areas of western Montana, unreachable by automobile.

The VA (Veteran's Administration) also tried every known experiment to try to cure my Tinnitus (ear-ringing,) without any success, so they took away the 10% disability after six months, amounting to five dollars a month.

I worked at this job for a year until the spring of 1957. It was probably the best therapy that I could have possibly had to get me mentally back on track and I have been ever grateful to Mr. Koga, John Satake and the Grace of God for sparing my life from going by way of the insane asylum at Warm Springs.

Johnny Ogata

Hi George, can you come and help me farm the ranch, my father was killed in an auto accident? That was the voice of John Ogata from Helena, Montana. By this time I had enough railroading and needed a change, so I agreed to come. Johnny by this time had gone to the La Tournneau Trade School for large earth moving equipment and was the best mechanic in Helena. He had built one of the finest farm machinery shops in Helena on the ranch and had the section of land under control.

We wanted to diversify and expand our resources so we leased another half a section of adjoining land, making nine hundred and sixty acres to farm. We had wheat, barley, oats, and pea seed for the cannery, alfalfa, potatoes, beans and row crop vegetable. This wasn't enough so John raised calves and George, being a pig farmer, raised pigs.

In 1947, to raise ordinary potatoes wasn't what we wanted to do therefore; we went to the county agent that put us in touch with the State College in Bozeman. He said that they had developed a new hybrid potato that had eight to ten perfect-sized baking potatoes per hill. They were supposed to be smooth skinned, shallow eyed and no knots. After talking to the professor who developed them we bought seed and planted fifty acres. Every two weeks the agent came out to check on them and they were producing right on schedule. The dreamland dollars were already stacking up in the bank as we eyeballed the potential. Harvest day rolled around, our trucks were all ready, new branded sacks were laid out and a crew of Indians from the Blackfoot Reservation was ready to start.

The harvesting got off to a great start, but the potatoes seemed to be getting bigger and bigger as we got into the mile long rows. It got so that the Indians couldn't pick the potatoes up because they were so large. Most of them were over three pounds each and like a football. Now what do we do?

The stores and the restaurants didn't want those big potatoes; the potato chip factory didn't have equipment large enough to handle them either. The Government inspector came out and sprayed the potatoes purple to designate them a culls. As a last resort we turned John's cattle into the fields, but the potatoes were so large that the cows could only lick them. Before we could disc them up into bite size pieces, the heavy frost came and we learned that there is a price to pay for greed.

Undaunted we went on to harvest the rest of our crops and sold our livestock to clear our debts from the potato episode and machinery repairing was thriving.

CHAPTER 7

Buttons and Bows

Eyes on a Dude Ranch

In late September 1947, a tempting letter from the Alexander's came in the mail from nice warm Tucson, Arizona. *"We have found a dude ranch for sale, it's fully equipped and doing well for a price that we can afford. Our plan is to pool our WWII resources, buy county land on the edge of the city limits and to build a modern duplex with high ceilings and new ideas to sell for a handsome profit. We have found some plans drawn up by an architect in Beverly Hills, CA. that look good. Mom, Toni, and the boys want you to join us. Can you come? Love Bill."*

"I'm on the way! Love George."

Tearfully, I packed up my stuff hugged my friend John Ogata and headed out for Tucson. As I drove along the icy roads through Idaho and Utah, it gave me a chance to visit old war buddies, Nelson Akagi and Jiro Tsukamoto and to catch up on post war life in the making.

Heading south with twenty-five year old stars in my eyes singing America's favorite catchy-tune, "Buttons and Bows," my trusty old Chevy coupe got me to Tucson without a hitch.

To be back in the arms of the Alexander's was like being in heaven and having my sanity back after the nervous break down was beyond thankful words. Mrs. A had broken her back in an auto accident and was on the mend in that climate. Bill was cheerfully in charge and overflowing with how the plans were working out. Just to look at gorgeous Toni was more than words could say and we didn't say much. She was working on her masters in education at the University. Jim was back to oil painting those beautiful horse scenes and dreaming of pack trips on the dude ranch. Doug was now huge in the saddle and eager to get with it. He and Jim had purchased a Dodge pick-up truck that was their pride and joy. Lastly, Ranny with his perpetual mile-wide grin between the freckles was enrolled in the University of Tucson.

Two other new people came into my life, "Granny," Mrs. A's mom from Belgium had moved in and her rosy cheeked grandson, "Jack" was with her. They were wonderful people and made the walls in the house bulge. Granny was in her seventies and Jack was a teenager enrolled in high school.

The outfit had rented a four-bedroom house on the edge of town that had a large adobe brick wall all the way around it. The back yard had a canvas-enclosed double bed swing that Bill and I shared. It was fun making plans and talking about our new horizons late at night when Toni and I weren't talking and laughing about the time when she told me that she had learned in an economics class that the stock market had taken a turn for the worse and that two companies that I had stock in., Continental Can Co. and Montana Gas & Water Co. were affected. She strongly advised that I hang on to the can and let my gas and water go.

Cooking for eight people was like being back at the boarding house in Bozeman and good training for the dude ranch. Our night meals were always a delight of teamwork and things to talk about. Afterwards before study time a ride down the old Sabino Canyon road in my coupe provided a few thrills and spills. On Sunday afternoons a trip to Sabino Canyon, to lie on the rocks and bask in the sun along the beautiful creek, pictured in the Arizona Highways Magazine, left more than footprints.

Our combined cash resources added up to about sixteen thousand dollars and the dude ranch was for sale at thirty five thousand dollars. Bill and the banker figured out that we could make enough profit on the sale of the two houses to easily accomplish our goals to get into business by summer.

This was my first experience with a desert climate and why people with arthritis, asthma and those escaping the northern winters come there for the winter. I also learned that this short window in time was called the "Tourist Season," and the population of the town more than doubled.

In what was called the "Off-Season," the local people lived there permanently for health reasons or were native Hispanics and ranchers. Tucson was a slow moving town in the off-season. The town was filled with every kind of small restaurants, boutique shops and saddle shops selling western type of art, jewelry and ranch needs. One in business depended on the tourist season to carry over the off-season.

Clearing Desert Land

Our first job was to clear our quarter of an acre of desert land and to make preparations for our new building. Out from under the greasewood bushes ran the red and black spotted Gila monsters, a desert lizard that is poisonous and has the urge to jump into a raging brush fire and dies. Not only were there Gila monsters but, scorpions, tarantulas, horned toads, sidewinder rattle snakes, roadrunners, and cutter ants that work in teams to cut the fresh leaves off of green plants, haul them off to their hole in the ground where they spit on the leaves that causes them to mold. They eat the mold for food and are difficult to poison.

In the desert, just a small amount of water will cause it to immediately start to turn green and all kinds of desert flora and fauna come to life. This was quite an experience for me to witness. The many varieties of cacti were a first for me to see and I could actually hear the giant saguaro cactus sucking up tons of water during a flash flood.

Arizona is made up of many dips in the highways, which are dry rivers or rivulets that become raging torrents during a storm. The sun baked dry adobe soil does not absorb water very rapidly so during the thunderstorms the water runs off and fills the dips to overflowing called flash floods. At this time the air is very electric and the sudden coolness makes one shiver along with the smell of ozone that is quite cleansing.

To watch the tiny little green leaves appear on the, dry-as-a-bone, ocotillo cactus stick-like plants, topped off with a tassel of red-orange colored long blossoms was breath taking. Not only was that of interest, but also the double "llo" in ocotillo is pronounced like a "ya" sound, which was so strange for me to adjust to. For the most part, Spanish was not that much different from the Italian language, which I learned in the military, but in this case it was awkward.

Cacti

A "jumping" cholla cactus bush is made up of many very fine, small spiny bulbous like nodules that grab onto anything that just barely touches it. Many times the bulb disengages itself from the main plant and gets entangled in ones clothing or it pulls one into the main plant if it does not disengage. The little spines are very venomous and sting and hurt a lot. It didn't take me long to show that plant a lot of respect and to give it a wide berth. When we cleared it from the land we had to make sure that we swept up real good under the plants and burned the droppings that seemed to stick to everything.

The giant saguaro cactus is strange looking single pillar-like plant, usually with one arm sticking out of one side and bent up at the elbow that is very characteristic of Arizona. The accordion-like, pleated skin allows the plant to expand during the rainy season and the inside of the plant is made up of multiple tubes that store water and gives the plant structural strength. Woodpeckers often make their nests inside of the plant because there are no branches or foliage to nest in. On the very top of the plant are cactus type of open blossoms that attracts bees and sap sucking insects and birds. Some plants grow to be fifty feet tall and two or three feet across. A large plant will suck up as much as sixty tons of water during a flash flood.

Desert Night Life

A t night the desert comes alive with coyotes, jackrabbits, field mice, kangaroo rats, horned owls and even ants that are not seen during the daytime. Desert sheep and goats are seen in the high places at long distances away. The Arizona wild pig is called a peccary and is very small, probably fewer than fifty pounds. They are sort of reddish in color and run in decade-sized herds. What I didn't know was that they are very dangerous and ambush and attack hunters with their little grunts and razor sharp teeth while running full steam ahead.

Our land not only had several varieties of cacti, it also had sagebrush, greasewood, mesquite, bird of paradise, and palo verde bushes that all had to be cleared off.

Caliche

After clearing the land for few days and chasing the fauna, we had to start digging a dry well for the septic tank, which by code had to be four feet in diameter and twenty feet deep. The first ten feet was pick and shovel digging through adobe soil and then we hit a four foot layer of what was called caliche that was white and resembled taffy in texture.

This unheard of substance sealed the soil from water penetrating through it and was almost impossible to dig with ordinary tools. You can be sure it soon inherited a few choice names besides caliche.

To compound matters, the rumors around the valley was that there was an ancient underground river running under the valley floor and that some people have been known to break through the caliche and disappeared into the cavern. I think that some wise guys thought that they would have some fun with those hicks from Montana.

After several days of not making any progress digging in the caliche, ole George decided to try a trick that he learned in the army drilling holes with dynamite for digging howitzer emplacements. What you do is to put a small lump of dynamite on the surface of the ground or rock and put a blasting cap in it with a fuse and then you put a cone shaped paper cup over it, at an angle and light the fuse. Bang! A nice round hole appears in the ground. After you drill several holes you fill them with dynamite and blow a big hole. Wow! It worked and our caliche problem was solved. No one fell into a cavern that wasn't there.

The Big Bang

The next project was to level the ground and put in a concrete foundation for the walls. We mixed our own concrete and poured it into the forms. This went along very well because Bill and the boys had learned to do that on the ranch and we even put up our own concrete blocks. The plan was to use radiant heated floors for the winter, so copper water pipes were laid out in serpentine fashion and concrete poured over them. Everything was on schedule and built according to the architect's plans. The sub floor was nice and flat and level and ready for the colored concrete floor to be poured, troweled and buffed to a high polish.

The day that we ordered delivery of the colored concrete it was unusually hot. The ready-mix concrete contractor showed up a few minutes early and the cement finishers showed up a few minutes late. Keeping a spray mist on the pour kept it from setting up but the finishers couldn't get the last room finished before the cement set up and it could not be troweled and buffed properly. Because it was dark and we could not tell how the job looked, we decided to let it go until the next day to evaluate the job. All but the last corner room looked pretty good, but the last room did not meet our approval. What to do was the question? We couldn't remove the concrete with ordinary tools and it was well bonded to the base concrete so, we rented a jackhammer and that went very slow. Someone suggested that we try the blasting technique and ole George shot a couple of holes and loaded a little too much TNT into the holes and when the big shot went off it cracked the outside wall and two top courses of concrete blocks fell down. Our schedule had now slipped a week and our materials budget took a beating. This didn't help emotions either, Bill was calm and cheerful but George, Jim and Doug were not.

Once that storm got over and the finish work inside got going again, the climate got better and we were all enjoying seeing results but everything seemed to take longer than we had planned.

Dell Webb Comes to Tucson

A real bomb landed on us when Dell Webb, the original tract developer showed up in Tucson and started to build cheap tract houses close to ours and the raw material prices took a steep drop.

Of course all of our material was purchased at the high prices. Real estate prices also took a nosedive and we could see our profits going south when those tract houses went up overnight.

One day a roofing salesman came by and gave us a demonstration on a highly reflective aluminum material that was easy to install and had three times the radiant heat reflectivity over other roofing and insulation material for one-half the cost. We opted to buy it and put it on.

It really worked well when the weather started to get hot until one day a couple officials from the county showed up and said that we would have to get rid of our roof. It turned out that our house was right in the flight path of Davis Monthan Air Force Base at Tucson and the pitch of our roof was such that the sun reflected off of our roof into the pilots' eyes, blinding them as they landed. There was an ordinance that prohibited any obstruction within the airfields airspace. We had to put on a non-reflective roof. By now our money was getting low and we were three months from completion.

By this time, Jim and Dooge saw the hand writing on the wall, loaded up their pickup truck and headed back to Big Timber, Montana to catch the summer haying and rodeos. When a dream turns into a nightmare what do you do but shake hands, hug and say good-bye.

The Cookie Business

What do you do when things get tight? You go look for a second job. Walking the streets of Tucson and neighboring towns, knocking on doors and reading the spots off of the want ads is hard work when it is the off-season and all of the jobs are reserved for the locals. One day it occurred to us that we would be cooking on the dude ranch so we decided to bake cookies and take them to the restaurants and grocery stores on consignment at twenty-five cents a dozen.

Every night we baked a hundred dozen cookies or more in our rented house and made deliveries in my coupe early in the morning.

One day someone asked if we catered weddings and we said, "that's our specialty." Mrs. A and Toni were fabulous with what they could do in the kitchen.

We made little finger sandwiches, punch and a four-tier cake with a fancy frosting etc. A whole bunch of eight inch white cakes arranged on a round piece of plywood covered with some fancy paper, followed by a second, third and fourth tier offset by eight inches per tier, makes an unusual looking cake. We all had a ball making the cake and decorating it.

On the day of the wedding Toni, Bill and I went to the church in our Levi's with holes in the knees and everyone was as happy as could be and paid us one hundred dollars.

California Here I come

July 1948 rolled around pretty fast and we were broke. Bill, Toni, Mrs. A and I discussed the situation and decided that I should go to California and stay with my friends and to get back into school under the GI Bill. In the meantime I took a drive out to some outlying towns in the desert and thought things over about my relationship with Toni and decided to end it because it wouldn't be fair for her to put up with any long-range plans with me. Bill would finish the houses, sell them, pay off our loan and also go back to school. Toni would graduate and have her teaching credentials to start in the fall.

Driving out of their driveway for the last time was as hard a thing as I had ever done in my life until then. All the way to California I felt worse than dying and I only remember going through Indio, California at night in 115-degree weather where my car boiled over and my feet got burned on the pavement.

The Saga of Dude Ranching

The saga of the dude ranching drama closes one of the most exciting and the saddest chapters in my book. Dreams turned into a nightmare of broken hearts, debts to pay, bittersweet relationships, shipwrecked and scattered by the winds of tyranny.

Bill finished the house, went to Pennsylvania to the same school that his father attended and became a doctor and got married. He later moved to Butte, Montana and became a shrink. The last time that I saw Bill was about twenty years ago when he came to see me and we cried a lot. Toni got a teaching job in Safford, Arizona and got married and had two children. Mrs. A. went to live near Toni and Granny died in her nineties. Jim was last seen in Big Timber and Dooge was living from job to job near Round Up, Montana. Ranny and his wife were living in Big Timber, Montana and came to visit me in California when their son got his doctorate at Stanford.

CHAPTER 8

Life in the Fast
Lane 1948

Welcome to Los Angeles

Welcome to LA, Mike Miyake said, when he and his wife May (Koga) came and rescued this brave warrior from the jaws of hell. Nothing was ever like this before and May and Mike had to orient this Oriental on life in the fast lane. Now I know where "Holy Smokes" came from. They were so very kind to me and let me stay with them while they taught me how to cope with LA before enrolling into school in August of 1948.

Rolling into Los Angeles on a Tuesday afternoon at 5:00 pm and ending up on Broadway Street, heading west looking for Sixth Street and getting scolded by a cop is not easy to forget. Signal lights on the street corners with an arm going up and down, a bell ringing, a colored light flashing, a big diesel truck gagging me with smoke and obstructing the names of the streets, was like jumping into a house of horrors at mid night. Through my tears I could make out a clanging streetcar coming down the middle of the street with one hundred-foot visibility in this new thing called SMOG that made matters even worse.

Somehow I managed to miss the streetcar and I had instructions from my friends May and Mike Miyake to turn left on Sixth Street. In a cold sweat Fifth Street finally showed up and I got in the left lane and put my arm out. Little did I know that at four o'clock they put a sign, mounted on a round metal pedestal, in the intersection that said "NO Left" with a cop standing behind it. My instinct was to follow the instructions or get lost in the big city. Wham, went the sign as it went rolling across the street, nipping at the cop's heels as ole George rounds the corner and all of the traffic comes to a horn-blowing, screeching halt.

"What in the hell do you think you're doing, came the whistle-blowing words into my ears as I skidded into the curb?" "Well sir, I was making a left turn according to my instructions."

"Where are you from?" Arizona." "Yes, I can see that from your license plate. Now you, turn around and go back where you came from and don't you ever come back!" "Yes Sir." I said as I headed to a telephone to call May and Mike.

Sometimes it is better to just sit still and peek out from under your arm once in awhile.

Cal-Aero-Tech

While you are going to school at Calif. Aero Tech. Institute, why don't you spend week-ends with us and help me and my dad doing landscaping work? When we are not working or going to the Ram's or SC football games you can play tennis with my wife Kay, were the words from my old Detail Section Buddy, Tahae (Tee) Sugita that came over the telephone.

Not wanting to get too heavily involved in engineering

subjects, I elected to rehab by taking a 2000-hour, intensive course in Aircraft and Engine Mechanics including overhaul and maintenance of Jet engines. Major Mosley, World War I Ace, who flew with Eddy Rickenbacher, started the school and The Grand Central Airport in Glendale, CA. This seemed to fit into my situation so I enrolled.

A classmate named Ariel and I rented a one-bedroom apartment with a kitchen in Glendale, CA for $35.00 a month and attended school eight hours every weekday for a year. Our classes included basic aeronautics, which I had taken in college; design and building of sub sonic air-foils; precision woodworking and finishing of all wooden aircraft parts; steel airframe design and hands on construction; electric arc and gas welding of both steel and aluminum tubing and plates; thermite welding; spot welding; aircraft weight and balance calculations; air cooled piston engine design and overhaul; liquid cooled piston engine design and overhaul; German Jumo Jet engine design and overhaul; General Electric Jet engine design and overhaul; fabric covered aircraft design and overhaul; plywood aircraft design and overhaul; control surfaces design and overhaul; aluminum structure design and overhaul; fastener design and selection; painting and finishing, instrument testing; engine test-stand rigging and testing; flight control rigging and testing; cabin pressurization; government periodical inspection and licensing of aircraft and engine requirements.

Highest honors were given to me when I graduated from this school and Major Mosley hired me as a special mechanic on his personal aircraft that I was responsible for maintaining and making design changes.

Tee and Kay and Butch

Weekends spent with Tahae (Tee) and Kaoru (Kay) Sugita were rewarding in every way. Even though landscaping was a fancy word for gardening and mowing lawns, it took us into the most luxurious and beautiful Beverly Hills, Hollywood, Santa Monica, Redondo Beach and Mulholland Drive estates. Tee's father was a very large man and was as gentle and nice as he was big so I looked forward to landscaping on Saturdays from daybreak to dark and coming home to Kay's delicious Japanese cooking.

Kay's brothers and their families the Emi's also lived in the same court. Frank shared with me the most difficult WWII days living in the Tule Lake Concentration Camp as one of the leaders of the "No-No" boys that objected to signing a loyalty oath after being denied his natural born American Citizenship. Tule Lake was the camp where the interns were mostly first generation Japanese emigrants under high surveillance. His Caucasian wife endured even worse traumas when she also lost her citizenship and lived with all of the Japanese people. Their two children were born in camp and didn't know much about the reality of it until they got out. Those talks revealed to me the stupidity of the whole affair that occurs when fear becomes the driving force of decision-making.

Kay had a lot of girl friends that she was continuously making connections with that included Miss Nisei Week Queen that were fizzles for this hayseed country boy. All day in gridlocked traffic on a narrow road getting to the beach, being all covered with sand, sticky from the salt and talking about local nonsense was not my idea of fun or romance.

My favorite rest time was watching a small black and white TV, which was a brand new invention for the times. It was so much fun watching wrestling on TV with Tee's father. Baron Leone was the big time villain and would make you love-hate him. After TV I shared the couch with "Butch," their Great Dane dog. It was always a toss-up to see who slept on the floor. My place was more often than not on the floor or under the big slobbering beast. It was a no-win situation, but the price was right and it included meals.

Tennis

Sunday mornings Tee slept in and watched baseball all day, while Kay and I played tennis or went horseback riding at Griffith Park. Kay was a champion on the tennis court and with her long straight legs and lithe body she would have me racing all over the court to win one out of three sets and I think those were gimme's just to keep me playing.

One fourth of July weekend, Tee and Kay took me to Pismo Beach to visit Tee's long time friends; the Ikeda family who had a produce farm and grew celery, corn, lettuce and strawberries. They put on a huge barbeque for the whole valley, which I thoroughly savored along with the introduction to Pismo clams and especially abalone, which you could catch in knee-deep surf.

Nami and Mitz

Another friend that they had in Pismo Beach was a big time, gentleman type of celery farmer named Mitz Sanbonmatsu and his wife's name was Nami.

We went to visit them to borrow tennis rackets so that Kay and I could play tennis. Wow, Nami was another knockout for looks. She had an old friend from the YMCA in Pasadena visiting her for the weekend named Mary Toyoda. We were introduced and casually said, "Hi."

Mary Toyoda

Mary Toyoda was one of six girls born to an immigrant Japanese farmer in Santa Ana, California. Her mother died at the age of two and was orphaned until she was eight years old. Katharine Weisser, her fathers' landlord adopted her at the age of eight and became to be known as "Aunt Kate." Mary grew up with Auntie's relatives the Weisser's, Lenhardt's and the Millers in Garden Grove, CA who became her best friends. They provided her with a family connection until she had to go alone into a concentration camp at Poston, Arizona even though she was in the hospital with pneumonia at the time. In that freezing cold wind swept environment she almost died but God spared her life and gave her comfort by continuing her violin playing at the Arizona, desert camp.

Mitz and Nami Sanbonmatsu and Tee and Kay Sugita thought that Mary and I should get together and urged us to do so, but neither of us agreed to that idea. Mitz and Nomi came to Pasadena to visit Mary and invited Tee and Kay and me to dinner out. Now obligated to them, in August I had to bite the bullet and ask Mary for a date to satisfy our friends so we went first cabin to dinner and to a play in LA that cost me a week's salary. To reciprocate Mary introduced me to her seventy-year-old, spinster, foster mother Miss Katharine Weisser and invited me to attend the Evangelical Mission Covenant Church in Pasadena. I really liked "Auntie," as she was called, even though she was in her seventies and rather stern looking. Going to church was no threat or objection to me, so I accepted the invitation.

CHAPTER 9

Reborn
[1951]

Arvid & Linnea Carlson

Arvid Carlson (RV) was the preacher at the Swedish Evangelical Mission Covenant Church in Pasadena, California and his wife's name was Linnea. I was quite impressed with Arvid's preaching, which was different than the usual run of the mill preachers. Mary played her violin quite often, which impressed me very much as well. The congregation, primarily Swedes, was very friendly and nice to me and I looked forward to going back.

I enjoyed the teachings twice on Sunday and sometimes on Wednesday evenings when speakers from the Fuller Theological Seminary, a few doors down the street filled the pulpit. These men were giants in their own specialties and very learned theologians. To name a few, there was Dr. Wilber Smith, my favorite who taught on Prophesy; Dr Karl Henry; Dr. Harold Lindsell, Editor of Christianity Today; Dr. Gleason Archer; Dr. Fuller and others.

Usually Sunday evening was less formal and Arvid would tell us application stories and a good joke or two dealing with life, which I really liked. He usually gave an invitation to become a believer and follower of Jesus Christ. I thought that I was already one so never responded.

One Sunday evening, after a fine supper at Auntie's house, we all went to church. Arvid started out by introducing a couple that had just accepted Christ as their Lord and Savior that day. He followed up by asking for a show of hands from those who had been "Born Again" one year and so on to fifty etc. When he got to five years my hand shot up based upon the event five years ago when Glen and I went into the little Church of Christ in Bozeman, Montana and went through the motions.

My already ringing ears came on like gangbusters and pounded until my head started to hurt. At this point, I came face to face with Satan, who was saying "Gottcha." All the way back to Auntie's house it was a very silent ride. I left and drove back to Glendale, got in bed and thought that I was going to have another nervous breakdown. I wrestled with the devil all night and woke up with my Bible reading a parable in Luke 8:18 where Jesus said, "take heed therefore, how you hear, for to him who has shall be given even more and to him who has not shall be taken away, even that which he thinks he has."

I thought that I was a Christian based on all of the knowledge that I had gained by going to church and from going through the motions at an earlier date. On Tuesday Morning March 13, 1951, I drove into Pasadena, kneeled in Pastor Carlson's office and invited Jesus Christ into my heart. Instantly a miracle happened and the ringing stopped in my ears and I could hear normally. Much to my amazement, a peace that passes all understanding flooded my soul and I was "Born Again."

From that day forward by the Grace of God, I became a new creature, old things passed away and all things became new. I eventually quit smoking because I wanted to and didn't need that crutch to sustain my life. My crude language diminished in the workplace and I wrote letters to every one of my old friends to tell them the Good News that Jesus Christ died on the cross to set me free from the bondage of sin and became my personal Lord and Savior.

Marriage

B y the Grace of God, Mary and I fell in love with each other and we got married at the Mission Covenant Church in Pasadena on August 26, 1951. We were as poor as church mice so Auntie was kind enough to let me move into their tiny two-bedroom apartment at 199 south Oak Knoll Street in Pasadena. By now, I was the working-night-foreman at the Grand Central Aircraft Company in Glendale with over one hundred men to manage. My salary was two dollars and eighty-five-cents an hour. I drove about twenty-five miles a day to work, which was a lot of miles without freeways. Tires only lasted ten thousand miles and engines needed complete overhaul every twenty or thirty thousand miles. Being a grease monkey with tools was a lot more important to me than a romantic wedding.

Working at twenty-five cents an hour as secretary to several Nobel Prize winning Nuclear Physicists at California Institute of Technology, Mary earned enough money to buy groceries and to continue to pay for her violin lessons. She also played her violin for the Pasadena Symphony Orchestra, which was within walking distance of Auntie's house.

Before we got married, I traded my treasured Chevy coupe and borrowed enough money to buy a brand new, four-door, six-cylinder Ford car for thirteen hundred dollars, including the spare tire which was a post war accessory. Our car payments were one hundred and thirteen dollars a month for thirteen months, the maximum loan period available.

That was about a full weeks salary before taxes. Just dating kept me eating grilled cheese sandwiches and Bob's Big Boy hamburgers. After buying a six hundred dollar ring set and new duds didn't leave any money for a honeymoon, but I was used to taking risks by now.

Roland Hipley, my good friend and co-worker consented to be my best man and his wife Pat was an encouragement to my shaky knees concerning the ceremony which I was not looking forward to. Just remembering when to say, "I do " was a big job. By this time I had only been to two other weddings, one being my roommate's formal Catholic wedding and my best friend, Sus Ito's wedding in Cleveland, Ohio. There was a whole lot different feeling being best man at a wedding or being the bridegroom. Having already experienced many trials of life, nothing seemed to prepare me for this event. After the vows and a quick reception which Linnea and Auntie put together with help from the church ladies, we jumped into our new car and headed north.

Our first honeymoon stop was at a motel in Ventura, CA and we nervously consummated our marriage. Our drive up Highway # One, through the amazing Redwood Forest into Oregon left us with so many wonderful memories and new adventures. Every day when we filled our gas tank the service attendants would spot our shiny new wedding rings and make comments. In Oregon along the Columbia River, we stopped at the Dalles and watched the Celilo Indians net huge fifty-pound salmon from frail scaffolding hanging over the falls. These beautiful falls where Lewis and Clark almost lost their lives disappeared when the Columbia River Dam was put in a few years later.

Arriving where Lewis and Clark had passed through this part of northwestern Montana was so vast and so beautiful that we stopped in the town of Salish where Chet Young and his wife Bertha were living and he was still working as the

Depot Agent on the Northern Pacific Railroad. Of course it was my pride and joy to showoff my beautiful new wife and to stay in their nice little guest cottage. They lived on the Salish Indian Reservation so we got to meet a number of people from that tribe of Indians. Many of them lived in teepees and spent most of their time gambling with a stick game that the women controlled. We hated to leave this dear couple and to drive about another two hundred and fifty miles to Logan, Montana.

Saved by Grace

Just before we got to Three Forks, Montana on Highway No.10, about fifteen miles from Logan, we were driving about sixty miles an hour, very close behind a bakery truck, whose ramp gate had come down and was bouncing up and down on the support chains. All of a sudden, without any warning the chain broke and the big heavy gate flew off and just cleared our car by an inch or two. That was such a close call from being wiped out, that Mary and I pulled over, hugged one another, prayed for a while and thanked the Lord for sparing our lives.

Not having been raised in the country as primitive as Montana, for Mary, Logan was not the greatest place to go on a honeymoon and to go fishing and camping especially when she had gotten cystitis along the way and had to go to Bozeman to see the doctor. Hip boots, a straw hat, a fishing rod, and huge squirming trout were a far cry from a typewriter, shorthand, Greek letters, Nuclear Physic terms, or a violin and a bow. A sleeping bag on the ground in a tent wasn't exactly her idea of marriage, but it made our minimal life in the city look like heaven when we moved in with Auntie on our return to Pasadena.

CHAPTER 10

The Curds and Whey of Marriage

Curds

Awkward has many synonyms that all apply when an adopted daughter and adopted son-in-law move into a spinster's apartment. There is something about roles and rubbing up against one another in tight quarters that change what had been smooth sailing, to eggshells for everyone involved, including the twenty–five pound kitty named "Toby." The kitchen and dinette was about six feet by ten feet with a stove, a Servel refrigerator, sink and dinette with three chairs and a back door. The bathroom was about four feet by six feet with a tub, sink, toilet and cupboard. Our bedroom was about eight feet by ten feet with small closet and double bed. Auntie's room was about ten feet by ten feet, leaving the living room about eight by ten feet with a front door and hall.

The nice thing about this house was that it sat on a three-foot hill above the street and it had a nice backyard incinerator, where you could burn anything until the Air

Pollution laws went into effect a few years later.

My working the night shift had its pluses and helped to make things a lot easier but limited our sack time together. It was nice taking Mary's lunch to her and eating it on the lawn on campus and getting to know her associates Bobby Spears, Jan Rasmussen and others. Some days we met church friends for a sack lunch some place in Pasadena. Arvid and Linnea let us stay in their parsonage, while they were on a vacation, which was a luxurious blessing from the Lord for us.

Here in Pasadena I discovered that my dear friend and Dean of Mechanical Engineering, Fred Homann had retired and we spent a number of quality days reaffirming our common ground of rejection by one's own country, he in WWI and me in WWII. I will never forget how much Fred did for me at Montana State College in Bozeman.

Whey

Near Pasadena was the Santa Anita Race Track. It was closed on Sunday and the huge 2000 car parking lot was empty, making it an ideal place to learn how to drive. For three Sundays, we took our new Ford car there for Mary to practice driving, which I thought would be a snap. After two broken sawhorse barriers, a smashed headlight, stripped gears and our first shouting matches, I decided to save our marriage and send her to driving school. Two weeks of intensive instruction led the instructor to cover up his head and opt for an automatic shift or quit.

An eight cylinder, automatic shift, Pontiac Catalina with a two tone green hard top, with real leather upholstery and only 3500 miles on the odometer came into our cash flow when the driving school instructor told Mary that, "If you want to drive a car you will have to buy one with an automatic transmission."

What an expensive and degrading option for me to have to give up a stick shift. But God, in his wisdom, graciously lead us by the hand to the Pontiac Agency in Pasadena where the dealer's wife, had just traded in her top of the line sports car for the new model. With our less than a year old Ford and nine hundred dollars we drove away in our classic new sports car with the works. To this day, sports cars, with automatic transmissions are all that Mary has ever driven and I, with tongue in cheek, love them. Of the twenty-five cars that I've owned in my life only five had stick shifts. We celebrated our fiftieth wedding anniversary this year, confirming that God knows best.

Rumble, rumble, rock and roll came the 1952 Tehachapi earthquake at about six o'clock one morning waking us up from a dead sleep. Toby's eyes as big as saucers were the first things that I saw and his howling was enough to wake up any dead person. Jumping out of bed, stark naked and trying to get under the bed in case of an earthquake as every one was told to do. When all of our wedding gifts were stored there, there wasn't any room for us. We couldn't go outside either, so we wrapped up in a blanket and stood under the doorjamb until the earthquake quit. To this day I don't remember trying to care for Auntie nor what she did. When all had quieted down and I put on some clothes, we discovered that our chimney had fallen off and the bricks were on our front porch where we would have been if we had run outside. Those are laughable realities of life that entertain our memory flicks.

Grover and Harriet Hayes

When I went to college I lost track of some of my high school classmates but somehow we learned that Grover Hayes had a watch shop at Nash's Department Store in Pasadena. Mary and I went down to the store to check it out and sure enough there was Grover behind the counter repairing and selling watches. He had his head down and didn't see us so we sneaked in. I put my head down and was looking over the watches, when he said, *"Can I help you with something?" Pointing I said, "I'd like to see that watch." "This one?" "No not that one." "Oh, this one?" "No, the one next to it." "Oh, okay."* By now all of the watches were on the counter and he was getting a little exasperated so I finally looked up and said *"Hi Grover."* After twelve years we looked the same and had a hilarious reunion.

Grover brought me up to date and I discovered that he and Harriet Price had gotten married and Dean Pogreba and Maxine Albro got married. I was shocked that they had switched partners from when we were in high school. He also told me that during the war he was a gunner on a B-27 Bomber and had flown and survived thirty-eight bombing missions. He joined the police force in San Louis Obispo, California and one night when he and his partner were playing draw with live bullets, his partner shot him in the rear end so he got into the jewelry business.

Anita Oiye

Then one day, our tent pegs were uprooted by the sad news that my dear friend and sister Anita who had been to the Mayo Clinic in Rochester, Minnesota was being sent home to Logan, Montana to die of intestinal cancer. Naomi was right there to comfort us and to encourage us on our decision to quit our jobs and go to Montana to help my parents cope with the terrible shock. We had barely been married eighteen months and I was only two years old in the Lord by then but we made the choice to follow our hearts.

We were well established in the church's newly formed new married group and were beginning to grow in grace.

This was a major trauma for Mary to deal with; it was not easy to pack up all of our things and to loan them to new friends or to put them in storage. Auntie's life was also being totally disrupted so she moved to Garden Grove, California to be near to her sister "Mom Lenhardt's." But, some how the peace of God came over all of us as we moved forward to God's calling.

Naomi Johnston came along side and said, *"As you leave us behind, the scripture says that wells of living water will spring forth from you into everlasting life."* I didn't know the depth of what she was saying until I held my sixty-pound sister's rack of bones in my arms as she went to be with the Lord. Almost immediately my mother and father accepted Jesus Christ into their hearts and were "Reborn." From that day forward, there was no end to the lives that their lives touched and ministered to until the Lord took them home.

Walk Your Talk

Naomi Johnston, our adult Sunday School Class teacher, stands tallest in my early Christian experience. In contemporary language she, "Walked her Talk." and radiated the character of Christ. I cannot thank the Lord enough for giving me such a role model and mentor, who helped my new life in Christ and our marriage to get started on solid ground.

Logan's Bible Study Center

Oiye's farm house became a Bible study center for the Earl Roadarmels, the Shannons, the Henry Sorensons, the Joe Hupkas and the Bill Hardings, who later bought an old Episcopal church that had been closed for thirty years. For the cost of fifty dollars, a small revival began in the

Gallatin River Valley and the church was full on Sundays during the summer. The pews sort of teeter tottered and the old pump organ needed repair but with it the Holy Spirit filled the place with joy. In the winter most of the people went to Bozeman or to Manhattan Bible Church.

Joe and Laura Hupka

While Mary and I were at Logan, Joe and Laura Hupka came into our lives. They were believers and followers of Jesus Christ as their Savior so an eternal kinship has grown from that meeting. Joe and Laura had purchased the mercantile store and post office from Joe and Nonie McQuillan and were raising their three boys and a daughter in Logan.

Early in the summer two girls, Verle Mills and Dorothy Chatham came to Logan to start an adult Sunday school through the Christian Professional Women's Society. They had cleaned up the old Episcopal Church at the end of town and came to the Hupka's store to see if they knew any one that had a bed that they could borrow. Joe and Laura had a spare double bed so Joe and I volunteered to carry it down to the church and to help them get set up. In a small town rumors and gossip travel faster than a bullet so Joe and I got accused of doing all kinds of things with those two nice looking young ladies down there at the church. Joe has since passed on, but Laura and the siblings still laugh about our bed episode while Al, her new husband just smiles while enjoying their lovely new home in Bozeman.

Bumbie

Bumbie was a bum lamb that George Fairweather, a sheep rancher gave to Mary to raise and it filled a few gaps and healed a lot of scars from having to live and work on a vegetable farm. If you have never worked from dawn to dusk, which is from four o'clock in the morning until ten o'clock at night in the summer months at Montana's latitude and longitude, hoeing and pulling weeds is worse than pulling wisdom teeth without medication. Mary like a good trouper gave it her best shot but I wiped away a lot of tears and pulled a lot of weeds to keep my mom from getting on her case. Not being able to cook was not exactly a plus in your in-laws house but, our hauling local flagstone rocks and building a huge beautiful fireplace and a new living room in the old storeroom seemed to cover a lot of shortcomings. Bumbie and George Fairweather were always a lot of fun and a comfort for her as well.

Mom and Pop Oiye

Mary and my father "Pop" became good friends and he would treat her like his own daughter.

She especially liked the tomatoes and corn that he raised and would eat them until she got sick. Trout that "Mom" cooked for dinner and breakfast are still Mary's favorites. On days when I would go to Bozeman I would take Mary with me and we would always stop at the bakery and bring home maple bars. My parents looked forward to an afternoon treat and break with coffee. It was almost like a ritual with us, which we enjoyed as much as the treat.

Pizza Pie

We had learned to like the popular pizza pie, as it was known in California. Mom and Pop heard about it so much that they wanted to try one. Bozeman had just started a pizza parlor so Mary and I, with great gusto and fanfare brought one home. My parents were drooling with great anticipation and when we opened it up; their faces dropped and Pop said, *"That's a Pie?"* Needless to say, they did not take to pizza and every time that we have one we see my dad's St Bernard dog eyes droop to the table and we laugh.

Fall came on like a polar bear and it frosted real heavy on Labor Day so we helped Pop gather up the winter veggies and stored them in the basement; took Bumbie back to Fairweather 's, with many tears; we packed up our car and headed home.

Alone at Last

Arriving in California started a whole new era in our lives. Reuniting with old friends, finding a new apartment of our own, getting reestablished and for the first time in three years living our own lives and getting to know one another.

In 1953, I applied for a development-engineering job at Cal-Tech's Jet Propulsion Laboratory at the end of Arroyo Seco Canyon and was hired to develop solid propellant for rocket engines. Mary was hired back to work for Nobel Prize winner Dr. Carl Anderson at Cal Tech and we were happy to be back in church with our old friends at the Mission Covenant Church.

CHAPTER 11

Aerospace
[1953-1972]

Solid Propellant Development

The Sergeant Missile was the second generation of the four inch diameter WAC Corporal Missile, developed by Cal Technical Institute at JPL (Jet Propulsion Lab.) It was eight inches in diameter, giving it four times more cross sectional area than the WAC Corporal. In comparison to the diameter of a Space Shuttle rocket engine, it is almost inconceivable that rockets are scaleable to that size. However, Solid propellant technology has been around for many years in gunpowder design and each little particle of powder is called a grain that may come in many shapes or sizes depending on the pressure and burning rate desired for the application.

A solid propellant rocket engine is one grain of powder that is called an end burner. It has a burn rate for a specific design size of nozzle whose burn time is a function of its length. Great care must be taken in the manufacturing of the grain to keep any bubbles or voids from forming within the mixture that will cause the surface area to change shape. Cracks are dreaded faults.

My job was to work with the grain design engineer to mix the rocket fuel mixture and to cast the mix into round right circular cylinders, much like baking an eight-inch long cake four inches in diameter in a vibrating vacuum-oven. When the grain was made and cured at a precisely controlled temperature it was cut up into various geometric shapes, on a band saw for testing. There were a total of six of us on the project performing various functions.

To determine the burn rate, seven-inch long strands, and one fourth of an inch in cross section were coated with an inhibitor that sealed the grain from the air. Each test strand was drilled at six-inches and suspended on a lead wire connected to a precision electric stop clock to determine its burn rate. Burn rates at minus 100 degrees Celsius and plus 150 degrees Celsius were also determined to establish parametric matrices.

To test its structural uniformity and performance integrity, two-inch long, four-inch in diameter discs, called "hockey pucks," were made and coated with an inhibitor except on the burning end. A starting fuse was installed with the end-burning grain in a highly instrumented firing-chamber on the test stand. Thrust and chamber pressure was measured with electronic transducers establishing parametric correlations with extremes of temperature. Sometime huge explosions occurred when the grain had non-uniform burn surfaces due to shock cracking at low temperature, or poor mixing and casting techniques.

All of these data were used to determine a final selection of designs for the scaling of solid propellant rockets and missiles. Some of the tests at White Sands, New Mexico were hilarious when the rockets blew-up on the test stand or fell over and spun around like firecrackers on the ground or chased people scurrying for cover.

Liquid Nitrogen a Toy

Liquid Nitrogen (LN$_2$) was used in large quantities for performing our experiments. At minus 273 degrees Celsius it is crystal clear and forms very mobile little droplets that scurry around on the floor as they warm up and evaporate. This phenomenon became a wonderful toy for the laboratory personnel; when we discovered that the abundance of four to six inch desert lizards became fascinated with the moving balls of LN$_2$. They would chase the liquid balls, pounce on them and get so cold that they went into hibernation. They would lie over on their backs on the pavement where it was nice and hot; when all of a sudden, like magic, they would come to life and go scurrying off into the bushes. This was so much fun that we would invite the rest of the lab over to see our latest discovery. One time we tried to hurry the process along and dipped one lizard into a Dewar of liquid nitrogen. That was too big a shock and it died.

The Cal Tech Jet Propulsion Lab (JPL) was very primitive and basic in operation. We machined rocket propellant without any safety precautions and dumped the scraps into a common wire caged incinerator about ten feet in diameter that was lit on fire every Friday night. Normally the propellant burned about like the paper except it had it own oxygen that maintained combustion. One week so much refuse got piled up on top of the propellant scraps that it prevented the gas from escaping freely and the pressure built up causing the propellant to burn faster and faster until the whole incinerator exploded and caused a brush fire up the canyon. No one was hurt and of course, the fire department started to apply some stringent safety rules to our laboratory.

Liquid Propellant Development

Welcome to hazard row! The Liquid Propellant development engineers of JPL had a row of test cells facing down the Arroyo Seco Canyon toward Los Angeles. This bunch of engineers and physicists were next door to our lab and worked with things like White Fuming Nitric Acid (WFNA), Red Fuming Nitric Acid (RFNA), Liquid Oxygen (LOX) and Jet fuel (JP4), and Unsymmetrical Dimethyl Hydrazine (UDMH).

Some days when they fired a RFNA or WFNA rocket motor, a huge cloud of very acrid white or orange-red cloud of toxic smoke would engulf our area and cause our eyes to burn and to gag us. On one occasion, just after a rainstorm, when the air was very heavy a large tank of UDMH sprung a leak and the entire campus was covered with a pale blue colored haze, about waist deep. Not knowing any better, everyone went walking around in it wondering what it was. Fortunately there were no open flames and a wind came up that self cleared the area.

The second year that I worked at JPL my eyes became dysfunctional and caused me to get dizzy spells. The eye doctor determined that it was the heavy smog in Pasadena that was causing it. Every morning we could watch the yellow bank of SMOG come rolling up the Arroyo Seco Canyon from Los Angeles and totally engulfed JPL by ten o'clock and linger until the evening breeze took it back to LA. The doctor sent me to eye training school everyday for a month to exercise my eyes until they would work properly. It seems that it was a common fault with young school children and they had special schools for them to attend. Sitting on the small chairs and using the small size stereoscopes was quite a novel event for the little kids to watch me struggle with.

By 1954 the city of Pasadena realized that the air

pollution was getting to be quite a problem and they abandoned the use of backyard incinerators and required JPL to haul their trash away to land fills.

Grand Central Aircraft Company

Mary and I decided to get out of that smoggy place and to give up our jobs with Cal Tech. With tears in our eyes we moved to Van Nuys, California where we bought a brand new house for eighteen thousand and five hundred dollars.

A new house with a seventy-five dollar a month mortgage, car payments, landscaping and fences to put in, and new furnishings to buy didn't leave us with any spare cash. Mary chose to go into selling Mary Kay Cosmetics and doing make-up on women. I went back to work for Grand Central Aircraft Company and was put in charge of the lines that built executive aircraft conversions. I also made aircraft parts in my garage and took night classes at UCLA. Some place in between I made our furniture that we kept for forty-five years.

Major Moseley was a very creative entrepreneur who purchased old military airplanes from the US Air Force, at scrap metal prices. We took DC-3s or DC-4s and made them into expensive plush aircraft. These airplanes had tail down landing gears and were awkward for women to get in and out of, so he invented what he called an "Air-stair-door," that would, at the push of a button, come out from the belly of the fuselage and the door would come open when the steps were in place.

Another of the Major's innovations was the full "Panorama Windows," for the cabin and the cockpit that allowed unobstructed low altitude view of the landscape. The cockpit windshield included a hidden frost-free hot air system, which I invented and the pilots loved.

Mr. Johnson of Johnson and Johnson Pharmaceuticals Inc. had us pressurize and convert a B-25 bomber into an executive aircraft with long-range fuel tanks and high altitude engines. This required taking out all of the armament, replacing all ribs and intercostals, replacing the skin and windows and basically making a new airplane that had a bomber silhouette. A full time shop crew of fifteen people and as many as fifty people from other shops worked on this project at one time.

The use of Plexiglas and Formica were becoming quite popular, state of the art decorator items and our wood shop became very good at custom building aircraft interiors to suit the customers whims. Lavatories, wet bars, and swivel leather-upholstered lounge chairs on sliding tracks with gimbaled cup holders and reclining footrests were standard amenities.

One of my jobs was to go to Hollywood, Beverly Hills and Santa Monica to buy exclusive fabrics and wall coverings for our projects. This was quite an experience going into those plushy places and learning about that trade. The first time that I went there it was rather embarrassing and awkward showing up in Levis and shop shoes. To be exposed to the prices that the other half paid for luxury was almost inconceivable for this ole farm boy.

Mr. Johnson told me that he only worked for himself the first four days of January and Uncle Sam took the rest, so he didn't care how much we spent on his airplane. As he and his secretary flew away in his new toy in less than two year's time, that was one happy executive having the luxury of owning his one-of-a-kind flying parlor.

Cinerama

MGM was making the famous movie "Cinerama," that revolutionized movie making and popularized surround sound. Paul Manse, who was flying a B-25 bomber for them, came to visit Major Moseley. He wanted to know if the Major would consider building the camera mounts in the Plexiglas nose dome of that bomber. I was given the project and had great fun making hair-raising trial runs with Paul Manse.

Curled up there ahead of anything else in the airplane was like riding a flying carpet with little noise or vibration from the propellers or engines. Flying through some of the local canyons and clouds along the California coast was breathtaking. Paul Manse did some extreme stunts to test the integrity of the camera mounts and I went along to see how we could improve any marginal design areas.

Cinerama shown at Grauman's Chinese Theatre in Hollywood is my favorite and the most impressive technical movie filmed in real time.

The expert use of state of the art cinematography and stereo sound equipment to give one the feeling of narrowly missing jagged Alps and skimming over the beauty of America was way ahead of its time in 1955. One of my favorite scenes is to see the bugs splattering on the Plexiglas dome flying at two hundred miles per hour. It also gave me a high regard and respect for the bomber gunners sitting out there all by themselves in an air raid, with only a thin sheet of Plexiglas for armor. At least a foxhole had dirt walls to hide behind and a place for your feet to feel the touch of earth hanging on to you.

Learstars

Unexpectedly and at a weak moment, Mr. Bill Lear made me an offer to come to Lear Aircraft Company in Santa Monica to help him convert twelve Lockheed Lodestar aircraft into executive planes called "Learstars." He put me in charge of interiors, which turned out to be an interesting job doing custom building on a production line. Just dealing with some of the wives on selection of decorations and décor required all of the skills that I'd learned from my previous trips to Beverly Hills.

The most interesting thing that crossed my plate while working for Bill Lear came when his wife gave me an assignment to do. Bill was pretty much of a ladies man and had flying lunches with a current girl friend almost every day; but it was no problem for his wife. She being a creative lady, decide to convert Bill's home den into a plushy room with all leather furniture and jazzy wall coverings. One wall in particular was covered with large professional black and white photographs of all of his known girl friends. Our interior shop personnel had a real bonus doing that one.

We never saw much of Bill Lear, but when our production line neared its completion he decided that he wanted to build a jet airplane called a "Lear Jet," so off to Germany he went with the intention of getting Willy Messerschmidt to build the engines for him. They could not come to an agreement so he went to France and got them to build the engine.

He asked me if I wanted to work with him on that one when he got his act together and in the mean time work on a steam engine car. Both jobs sounded intriguing but that long drive over Mulholland Drive (death row Canyon) was too stressful to drive and I wanted to get a degree in Aerospace and Rocket Engineering so I opted to quit and go to work for Lockheed Aerospace Company in Van Nuys, my hometown.

Lockheed Aerospace Company

The lure of Aerospace kept ringing in my ears as I joined Lockheed and was assigned to do the mechanical packaging of a thirty-two-channel telemetry system within a four-inch diameter missile. The sounding-missile gathered real time design data for the Atlas Missile then on the drawing boards. This package of self-contained modular electronic gear had to fit within twelve inches of allotted length and pass the entire design requirement of aerospace environmental tests.

Chuck Goedecke

When I met the project engineer, I was shocked. How many Chuck Goedecke' s are there around? It turned out that Chuck was my classmate at Montana State College and was the smartest electrical engineer in the school. We had no other close relationships because electrical people and mechanical people were two different kinds of engineers. This project took every skill and innovation that we could muster up to put that ten pounds of stuff in a five-pound pail and make it all work. I sure learned a lot about miniaturizing electronics and stretching my thermodynamic boundaries of mechanical engineering. What was even more ironic was that ten years later when I bought a house in Los Altos, California, he lived across the street.

The biggest thing that stretched my patience and relationship with the Lord was a phrase called, "This is a Union Shop." Engineers were not unionized and liked to get their hands dirty so the oil floated to the top and I was forever into trouble with the water of the establishment. Once I came in at night to check on my project and turned-on the lights. The whole program got shut down until the grievance committee took action for my taking away a union worker's job.

One other thing that intrigued me was that a ram jet engine was used on the drone that carried our missile into the upper atmosphere. Our neighboring company, the Marquardt Aircraft Company, made the ram jet engine.

Near the completion of this project, the Lockheed

Aerospace Company decided to move north to unheard of Sunnyvale, California. All employees were invited to move and retain their jobs. I was considering the option but, my wife had a job working for the president of a newly formed Company in Pacoima California near Van Nuys called American Machine and Foundry Company (AMF.) They had an Air Force contract building an Accessory Power Unit (APU) for the Atlas Missile and she didn't want to move.

Test Engineer

George Carver , chief engineer at AMF, heard from my wife that she didn't want to move to Sunnyvale and he invited me to his house for an interview. He was putting together a team of engineers to work on the Atlas Missile Accessory Power Unit (APU.) George had worked for Lockheed during WWII and subsequently at the Marquardt Aircraft Company. With my education and all of the aircraft and missile experience that I had, he hired me without any questions as a test engineer to work for Charley Mayo whom I had never met.

George was a very low key, laid-back pipe-smoking thinking individual who had literally lived in old engine crates during the war and later built his own twenty five hundred square foot house out of hand made adobe bricks. In doing so, he started an adobe brick manufacturing company that did quite well during the post war years when adobe brick houses were popular. He used the big hole in the ground next to his house, where the adobe came from, for a gunited concrete swimming pool. One of the other firsts for George was to build a camper out of a VW Van, which became very popular and also became a small business. All of the side businesses were done while working for Lockheed or Marquardt.

In those days, the office called, "Personnel," was more of

an administrative office that kept employee files and the various bosses could hire and fire people on their terms. What is now called Human Resources (HR) carries a big book and nothing happens, regarding employees, without them.

Today a boss walks on eggshells and needs a lawyer's council before opening his mouth. Thank God, my working life was lived without rules or limited rules before HR or Ralph Nader's OSHA. These are both good offices, but too restrictive for a farm boy's way of survival by an idea, a handshake and by the seat of the pants.

For me to survive, I never knew that *"It can't be done'"* or *"It Won't Work,"* ever existed until the textbooks or some philosopher said so. With God, *"All Things Are Possible, and Can Be Done."*

The APU was a self contained modular package that provided eight minutes of DC-electrical power; four hundred cycle AC-electrical power and 2000 psi hydraulic pressure to the missile during initial start-up and launch phases. This machine used the missiles JP-4 Fuel and Liquid Oxygen (LOX) oxidizer to drive a simple six inch, hot gas, impulse turbine to drive a gear-box running at a constant speed. The speed control was a frequency modulated electronic system that sensed the electrical frequency for reference and in-turn controlled the turbine speed by modulating a resistive load bank according to the missile demands. The fuel and oxidizer mixture was introduced into the turbines combustion chamber through a dual valve called a composite valve. This mixture was very precisely regulated by fixed valve-orifices before being ignited by a standard glow plug in the combustion chamber.

The Chicken Coop

A whitewashed converted chicken coop was an interesting place to have a high-tech engineering office and laboratory. It was a one story wooden building that had about 3000 square feet. It housed about forty people, shops and small test labs. The main test lab for testing was later built out of a converted pre-stressed concrete, bunker used in WWII by Lockheed Aircraft Company and given to us for free. At one end of the building was an inside staircase that went a half story up to a chicken coop. The location of the facility was next to the flood control, percolating reservoir, a barren gravel bed at Pacoima. The first year that I was there we had an un-seasonal amount of rainfall and the dam almost overflowed on us.

Charley Mayo

Charley Mayo, my new boss with red hair, a matching fiery temper and a string bow tie was the first person to came into my life at AMF. He was in charge of the test labs and had already hired Carmine Master, instrumentation engineer; Bill Escobar, test engineer; and Kenny Yap, test equipment design engineer. These three engineers were already cramped in the half story attic of a chicken coop and I showed up as a test engineer to further cramp the space problem, so George Carver and Charley Mayo had words. You never win with George Carver so it was now Charley and George Oiye. The cigar smoke from all of the smokers down stairs concentrated in the ventless, windowless attic, clouding the issues even more. Fortunately, the four of us sardines, hit it off real well from the word go and strong bonds began to build between us.

When a new kid shows up on the block and your boss dumps him on you, the wagons have to circle for a while to size one another up. Neither Charley nor I are very good communicators, so getting started was a bit strained under the circumstances and I changed jobs after a year. Just so that you know the rest of the story, Charley is one of my best friends at this writing, but not without conflict along the way. He is the most loyal friend to all of the people that he hired and that worked for him that I know. My pastor once said, "One thing for sure is that when Jesus is in the boat, the boat won't sink, and the storm won't last forever."

Carmine Master

My first job was to work with Carmine Master to join and enclose the two halves of the concrete test cells for development and production testing APUs. We installed and instrumented the control room, which was located between the two test cells with sixty-four channels of high-speed oscillograph strip chart recorders that worked with a Wianco analog system that was the state of the art electronic data collecting systems. It was not without development problems getting all of the pressure gauges to respond and function correctly through out the tests especially during the start-up transients. Carmine had a full staff of electronic and instrumentation techs and I had a full staff of mechanical techs to do the dynamic and static testing.

Putting in a window sized periscope for viewing the live tests was quite sensational and successful in spite of the difficulties cutting through the tempered concrete walls. In retrospect we have said that we would have saved a lot of money and time if we had built the concrete bunkers from scratch instead of trying to make a silk purse out of sows ear. Bill Escobar was responsible for the test cell plumbing, electrical raceways and test cell equipment.

When the floods came we waded around the test cells up to our knees in cold water while putting together the first Schlieren system for photographing and measuring hot gas nozzle velocity in the supersonic range. This was an invaluable engineering job for developing the turbine blade angles and speed control that used a precision ground, front-surface mirror that translated the second derivative image of the shock angle to velocity by refracting the varying densities of the hot gas impinging upon a known sharp pointed tungsten cone angle.

Carmine got a phone call when we were working on a test set-up and he disappeared for days. His son had drowned in a swimming pool and the entire test lab went into shock and mourning. Thereafter, many nights we didn't go home when an important test was running and we all slept on canvas cots in the test cells, much to the chagrin and strain on our young wives. Charley Mayo was very unpopular with wives during those long days.

Carmine and I also went to night school working on our professional engineers licenses along with many long hours of grueling work. The three of us have kept up our long-term friendships for almost fifty years in many ways.

Kenny Yap

Kenny Yap was a special Asian guy who had lost an arm in the war. With his prosthesis arm, he could do more things with it than the rest of us could with two arms. He did the three-dimensional layouts for all of the test set-ups and test cells that were exacting and always on time. None of us know his whereabouts today as he sort of disappeared when AMF later on merged with Sundstrand Turbo Corp. Not only was Kenny a good design engineer, he was a good man to emulate. In his own quiet way, he helped to keep our chicken coop from loosing its feathers many times. When an Air Force test plane narrowly skimmed over our test cell and crashed into a school yard nearby, Kenny and I were standing on top of the test cell and were so close to being hit by the plane that we could see the terror in the eyes of the pilot and copilot just before their deaths. This incident shook up the whole San Fernando Valley and LA Basin.

Here again he remained cool and collected, while I did my share of shaking.

Bob King

B ob King, being a Montanan and better yet from my old Alma Mater in Bozeman worked for George Carver. He was responsible for mechanical design of the APU hot gas generating system and valves. Very little or nothing was known about cleanliness of oxygen handling equipment and its incompatibility with oil and grease. I worked very closely with Bob and his mechanical tech testing valves and regulators. Until we learned that all oxygen handling equipment had to be 100% oxygen free, several near miss explosions occurred in the test cells, resulting in making everything out of squeaky clean stainless steel with specialty inert seals and diaphragms. We worked very closely with component vendors to develop exactly what was needed for a fail-safe operating system. Test personnel had to make sure that they didn't use any oil or grease in their hair to make sure that their hair didn't catch on fire around the large quantities of oxygen that we used.

Bob was very skillful working with the Air Force and with vendors to accomplish his goals. Several years hence, our kinship and compatibility lead to starting a company called King Nutronics Inc designing and building Aerospace Test Equipment in the LA Basin.

Time Out for Kids

O n the 5th of May in 1956, Mary and I went to our favorite ice cream parlor in Van Nuys and had a hot fudge sundae that started birth contractions and twenty-four hours later our son Tom was squeezed into this world. It was not an easy delivery and they didn't have the modern method of the husband sitting with his wife and helping her to breathe, etc. When we first saw Tom we were both worried that he would have a pointed head and look like an onion, but somehow God in his wisdom and grace worked things out, including the colic problems.

Thirteen months later, on the 20th of April 1957, Mary and Tom and I went to our favorite ice cream parlor and what do you know, contractions started again and this time our beautiful daughter, Nancy was born normally within eight hours. The only problem was that the outside temperature was over 110 °F and she had a terrible case of heat rash. We couldn't afford any air conditioning so a fan had to suffice. Every year thereafter on Nancy's birthday the weather in California has been hot, except in the last few years. Both of the siblings became believers and followers of Jesus at an early age and attended the Van Nuys Baptist Christian Day School for three years before enrolling in public schools.

The Marquardt Aircraft Company

The Marquardt Aircraft Company of Van Nuys, California had a position open for a ram jet engine development engineer to work on the Bomarc Ballistic Missile. I was intrigued with the concept so applied for the better paying job. This tactical, supersonic-missile was built by the Boeing Aircraft Company and the Marquardt Aircraft Company provided the engine. The ram jet engine took the missile to its flight path apogee at supersonic speed. When it used up its fuel supply the missile became ballistic. The ramjet engine was ideal for this application because in theory, the faster a ramjet flies the faster and higher into the troposphere it can fly because it depends on its forward velocity to get enough compressed air to sustain combustion.

When I got the job and resigned from AMF, Charley Mayo and I became the best of friends and our two families grew up together hunting and fishing every weekend and on holidays, in the high Sierra Mountains or on the Pacific Ocean.

Roy Marquardt

Roy Marquardt was a retired professor of aeronautical engineering at Cal Tech in Pasadena when he started his company in Van Nuys building ram jet engines. By the time I started to work for the company the state of the art for ram jet engine technology had advanced to supersonic aerodynamics requiring extremely sophisticated fuel control systems. A far cry from the ones used on buzz bombs by the Germans in WWII.

My first encounter with Roy was one week-end when I came into the plant to do some testing and I met this scruffy looking older guy tinkering around at an electronic bench humming to himself. I introduced myself and foolishly challenged his being there. He said, " Oh I was just tired of staying home and came in to find something to do. I'm Roy, nice to meet you and what are you working on?" I'm working on the fuel control system for the Bomarc." "Good luck, that's my latest hair-brain." I said, "Thank you Mr. Marquardt," as I slinked off into the shadows of the big blow down tanks.

Ram Jet Fuel Control Valve

Working with a fuel control valve with four inch diameter ports that used five servo-valves to control the fuel flow was more than a challenge when I had to go to school to learn La-place transforms and differential equations just to understand what my control and accessory peers were talking about as they wrestled with integrating mach numbers and shock waves at the entrance to the engine with the fuel control servo system. My job was to build the test stand hardware, test the fuel control valve to determine what changes needed to be made to accomplish our design goals.

The test set-up for testing the huge ramjet engine required using a General Electric turbo jet engine, from a Boeing 707 Jet airplane to provide the initial starter for the ramjet. A vertical tank farm consisting of twelve, about fifty foot long by ten feet diameter cylinders at medium high pressure, provided about three or four minutes of screaming, earth shaking, supersonic airflow to the ramjet engine. When running this engine made a humongous roar and exhaust flames that rattled the whole town of Van Nuys and beat on one's chest during the test. This was an awesome test and the city of Van Nuys and surrounding neighbor-hoods protested greatly. They eventually had the plant shut down for disturbing the peace and for noise pollution.

Sputnik and the Rise of Martin Luther King

Two little events that happened during this historical time period were the Russian launching of the "Sputnik Missile" and the rise of Martin Luther King. Charley and Marie Mayo and my wife, Mary and I were at the Ram's vs. Army football game in the LA Coliseum when some pranksters launched a giant helium balloon captioned "Sputnik" that floated right over the football game and made huge headlines in the LA Times.

Gordon E. Lee

One of my engineering buddies and officemates was Gordon E. Lee; every morning we got up at three or four in the morning and either played tennis or went bow and arrow deer hunting in the mountains by Sherman Oaks before going to work at Marquardt.

Gordon bought a war surplus Garand M-1 rifle and asked me to teach him how to use it. Being a good buddy I took him to the San Fernando rifle range and we spent many hours of instructions. Two weeks later Gordon quit his job at Marquardt and disappeared. We later learned that Gordon had gone to Montgomery, Alabama with the intention of killing Martin Luther King. None of us ever paid any attention to his name or knew that he was a direct descendant of General Robert E. Lee or that he was a racist at heart. I was especially relieved that James Earl Ray confessed to the assassination of Martin Luther King rather than Gordon E. Lee, but I still don't feel good about training him in the use of a rifle.

Sam Ostrow

Sam Ostrow an ex-Marquardt employee and friend of Charley Mayo called me and wanted me to come back to AMF, which had merged with Sundstrand Turbo Corp and was building a whole new facility for final development and building of the production version of the Atlas APU. Since the handwriting was on the wall for Marquardt and the fuel control system was working well I decided to rejoin my old friends at AMF.

AMF had the luxury of being spoiled by the Air Force, who had deep pockets at that time in history. They were just starting to work with the General Electric Company, who was designing the management systems for NASA. There were times when we couldn't spend money fast enough and many extra projects and tests were performed. State of the art shock and vibration equipment for components and system testing was installed at our test site. A full sized steam ejector plant was built to reach fifty thousand feet altitude in thirty seconds while running an entire APU system for eight minutes in the vacuum chamber.

The Borg Warner Company

A llan Puder, operations manager of the Borg Warner Co in Burbank, California was supplying AMF with the dc-generator for the APU, so we became good friends. After I had been with Sundstrand Turbo about a year, Allan got a contract to build the entire ground-test electrical load system for the Bomarc Missile and wanted me to head it up. That sounded like a lot of fun so I took him up on the assignment and went to work for Borg Warner.

Brushless-Permanent-Magnet-Alternators

B rushless-permanent-magnet-alternators was a new word and technology for me to learn as were magnetic amplifiers and saturable core reactors used for frequency and current control of the missile test equipment. It was my good fortune to meet Ralph Marshall, Lloyd Ott, Bill Douglas, and Lou Black all Cal Tech Graduates and experts in their fields.

I put in many long hours learning and applying these technologies. When it came time for the qualification tests to government specifications, Boeing sent their project engineer to buy off the equipment. Afterwards we all went out to "The Steak House," in North Hollywood, the best place in town to celebrate. I finally got home about three o'clock in the morning. The lights were on and Mary was still up so I asked her how come, and she said, "Oh, I just couldn't sleep." She then said how come you are so late?" I related the story of the circumstances and she said, *"What did you eat?"* When I said, *"Steak,"* she burst into tears and I was stumped. Through the tears she bawled,

"It's our anniversary!" Duhhh! Last Year was our fiftieth.

Lartec Inc

Lloyd Ott, Allen Puder and Ralph Marshal had started a little company called LARTEC Inc making electrical and electro-mechanical products. They wanted me to join them working nights and weekends machining parts and coming up with ideas. Lou Black had his own company making electronic control systems, magnetic amplifiers for deep-sea underwater treasure and sunken ship exploration. These were all very talented and interesting men that have connected in many ways over the years.

As a result of the success of the Bomarc test system we developed the first a-c sixty-hertz camper type of generator using permanent magnet, brush-less alternators and gasoline engines. Sears was our big customer and thousands of the units were sold. The Japanese were quick to pick up on that idea and soon captured the market.

King Nutronics Inc

In 1958 Bob King had been working, out of his garage building test equipment for aerospace companies in the LA Basin. One day in one of my weak moments, Bob asked me if I would come and start a company with him called King Nutronics Inc in Van Nuys. His parents were of the famous King Ranch in Lewistown, Montana and his mother had a USC alumni connection with both John Wayne and the lawyer for the Ford Motor Company, who had named the Ford Motor Company's Aeronutronics Division in New Port Beach, CA. The legal and financial worlds were not my forte so that would be Bob's area of expertise. My expertise was engineering and operations management.

We needed thirty thousand dollars to get started.

His parents and their haberdasher friend in Lewistown put up the money and drew up all of the paper work. Bob and I took big salary cuts and agreed to work for next to nothing. We leased a building next to the Schlitz Brewery and saw the sun come up every morning as we went home, showered, and went back to work.

Within a year we had over twenty employees and contracts with the Navy, the National Bureau of Standards and every aerospace company in the LA Basin. The United States Government Small Business Administration had registered us and gave us management and financial support. Aerospace companies were springing up and expanding almost everywhere. Our good friend Charley Mayo had moved to Orange County and was now working for Ford Aeronutronics heading up their test lab. He gave us several contracts to build equipment and Allen Puder and Ralph Marshall, whom now worked for Aerojet General in Azusa, gave us contracts as well.

One of our real triumphs came when the Secretary of the Navy telephoned me, on the last day of the fiscal year, to tell us that we had won a government contract, over Vice President Hubert Humphrey, to build large equipment to clean aircraft oil coolers for the US Navy and Marine Corp all over the world. This large contract was supposed to be an on-going shoe-in for the VP's company in Minnesota, but our long nights and sharp pencils did the job. It was a big job and required a lot of clever innovations to produce a better and more cost effective machine. We delivered on time and within budget, as well.

Tora, Tora, Tora

Church was an important part of the equation that we never lost sight of and by this time our family of a three-year-old son and two-year-old daughter were members of the start-up church in Panorama City called Grace Community Church, where we continued to attend until we moved to Tustin in 1966. Of interest is this little anecdote that happened in that church. Since I was an active elder in the church we always sat on the front row with our kids. Captain Mitsuo Fuchida was a very famous pilot in WWII because he led the attack on Pearl Harbor on December 7, 1941. One Sunday evening he came to our church to give his testimony on how he became a Christian. In a nutshell, after Pearl Harbor many incidents happened in his life during the war where his life was miraculously spared. When he was Japan's Minister of Air Defense he went to Hiroshima when it was bombed and was unharmed when he walked in the radioactive environment. When the war ended he took part in the signing of the peace treaty on the battleship Missouri and later became General Macarthur's right hand man.

Another man named Jacob DeShazer, a Doolittle-Raider-Navy pilot who was shot down, imprisoned and beaten hated Japanese people. He vowed to go to Japan and kill everyone, if he lived. DeShazer read the Bible in prison and was miraculously saved. His hatred turned to Love and he now vowed to go to Japan and evangelize Japan, if he lived. While standing on a street corner in Tokyo, Captain Fuchida came by and took one of the tracts that he was handing out. He was intrigued by this US Navy pilot who, like himself, miraculously survived the ravages of war and who became a Christian, thus resulting in Fuchida being converted. Capt Fuchida vowed to come to America to evangelize America, which he did.

When Fuchida finished giving his testimony we were the first to greet him and said. *"Do you have a place to stay?"* He said, *"What is your name?"* I said, *"Oiye san."* He proceeded to tell us that he had just come from the Manhattan Bible Church in Manhattan, Montana and an old

Japanese couple with the same name said exactly the same thing. Needless to say tears of joy flowed freely when I said, *"That's my parents."* While helping General Macarthur write his memoirs and participating in making the movie "Tora, Tora, Tora," we remained close friends until he died in 1969.

SNAP-8

B ombs not only fall in war, but some fall in our lives as well. Two blocks from our house, on the way to work, some teen-aged boys ran a boulevard stop going very fast and I hit them broadside. They had a large pick-up truck and my small English Ford was demolished. I landed on my head on the pavement resulting in a severe brain concussion, loss of memory, loss of taste, disoriented sight, aggravated ear ringing, broken ribs, kidney damage and ultimately loss of my share in the company.

But, by the Grace of God and my friends, I made a partial recovery within six months. Allen Puder and Ralph Marshall needed me to work on a high temperature, high-speed permanent magnet alternator to be used on the nuclear powered space station called SNAP-8.

I eventually became the project engineer for what was called the "Turbo-Alternator Assembly." This was a one-kilowatt, 400 Hz, four hundred forty volt, four pole, brush-less, homopolar, inductor, that was driven by a five stage mercury vapor condensing turbine. The equipment had to operate at full power continuously in a ten to the minus eight hard vacuum, for ten thousand unattended hours. The bearings and seals were dynamic molecular pumps designed and built by the General Electric Company in Schenectady, New York and the General Electric Company in Erie, Pennsylvania built the alternator. The alternator rotor weighed about fifty pounds and was lubricated with synthetic oil that would not evaporate at ten to the minus tenth vacuum pressure.

The five-stage mercury vapor turbine was made from Haynes twenty-five cobalt-nickel alloy using curvic-couplings between the stages to allow for the temperature changes. The blades were electro-discharge-machined (EDM) due to the hardness and brittleness of the material and to provide smooth flow paths. The turbine ran at 12,000 rpm whose speed was controlled by General Electric Company electronic controlled saturable core reactors that modulated the power going to a dummy resistive load bank panel in outer space.

The total weight of the turbo alternator assembly was four hundred and fifty pounds and was trunnion mounted into the airframe of SNAP-8.

For two years, one week out of every month I traveled to Erie, Pennsylvania, to Schenectady, NY and to Charlotte, NC to qualify the system by 1965. The equipment passed all tests and was qualified, but it never got to fly because SNAP-8 was shut down for its large budget over-runs, technical problems with the reactor and some of the other components.

Ralph and Mary Lou Marshall

All during the SNAP-8 program I drove from Van Nuys to Azusa, CA a round trip of sixty miles via Pasadena, where I left my car and shared a ride with Ralph Marshall. Ralph lived in one of the old mansions on Orange Grove Avenue where the Rose Parade floats were assembled. My family used to stay overnight on New Years Eve and walk around viewing the floats as they were being made. Ralph also had a fine engineering library and office in one of the upstairs cupolas, where we spent many late hours designing and working on engineering problems. Mary Lou, his wife was an elegant lady whose father was an admiral in the Navy during WWII. She was a widowed schoolteacher and had two children when she married Ralph and he had two teenagers as well. The hippy generation was in its infancy and Christopher, one of the boys made the cover of Time magazine when the students at Cambridge burned the school. So, you see there were many sagas of the Marshalls raising their kids to supplement our engineering problems and to add a lot of interest to life.

It was a sad day, when both of our jobs ended at Aerojet General in Azusa; Ralph went to work for the AEC in Idaho Falls, Idaho and became quite famous for his work on nuclear power systems, including investigating Chernobyl in Russia. I moved to Orange County and went to work for Aeronutronics in the ATC Laboratory. Many of the Aerojet technical people also went to work with George Carver and Charley Mayo at Aeronutronics in Newport Beach.

Shadrach, Meshach, and Abednego

Paul Stahlhuth, my good friend, a turbine and rotating machinery engineer from Sundstrand Turbo and I were assigned to Warren Kaufman, who worked for George Carver. Charley Mayo was in charge of the ATC test lab and Carmine Master and Sam Ostrow worked for him. We bid on and won a contract with Lockheed Aerospace, in Sunnyvale, CA to build a hot-gas turbine driven Hydraulic Power Supply (HPU) for the Poseidon Missile. I also bid on building the test consoles for qualification testing of the HPU at both facilities. My job as principal engineer was to head up a full project team of seven engineers and three techs. Paul was the lead project engineer and we made weekly trips to Sunnyvale to coordinate the program with Lockheed and spent many strenuous hours in motels keeping our project on track with our counterpart Russ Cloud, at Lockheed who was also a Sundstrand transplant.

As a bit of humor, three of our team members had unusual names like *Stahlhuth, Smisek, and Polzien;* whenever the going got heated, we would all laugh and say, *"Shadrach, Meshach and Abednego have been thrown into the fiery furnace again."*

Paul did such a fine job of designing and building the HPU that it passed all qualification tests, but when Lockheed awarded their production contract; the competition won. Our beautiful unit and project ended up in the surplus store with a broken heart. But, even though we won the battle and lost the war we said that God must have bigger and better things for us to do.

On my last flight to Sunnyvale a ten-year-old girl sat next to me and asked Jesus to come into her heart that was reward enough for me.

Quick Turn

After that Paul and I got locked up with a team of engineers for three months to design a quick-turn missile for use on the F-15 fighter jet. The week before Christmas the Air Force announced that our proposal had won but we lost the contract to the Navy. It turned out that the Department of Defense decided that the Navy's existing quick turn missile for the F-14 was good enough and that they shouldn't spend the additional money for another Air Force model. Another battle won and another war lost.

That meant, back to the drawing board for Paul. He got reassigned to Sheldon Hyman to build hot gas valves and rotating machinery for Lockheed until he retired and continues to build and fly RC aircraft and to walk with the Lord. Warren Kaufman, our boss went to Dearborn, MI and designed high performance fuel systems for the Ford Motor

Company, George Carver went into the sailboat building business and Charley Mayo went into business for himself building crates and has become very successful away from the phony corporate world.

My work at Philco Ford continued on in rotating machinery until I completed building and testing an experimental graphite turbine that successfully ran on six thousand degrees hot gas. This was a contract that we had with the US Air Force Materials Lab in Dayton, Ohio. I don't think that they ever built anymore of these machines but the technology learned was applicable to many hot gas applications.

During the War in Vietnam, the Ford Motor Company supplied a forty mm rotary mortar that was fired from a helicopter. This weapon was not too effective because the rapid-fire recoil caused the helicopter to vibrate excessively and spray the bullets with no accuracy. I was given the job of soft mounting the weapon to eliminate the vibration. This was great sport building a complete facility overhanging a bluff at our firing range at Capistrano, CA. The soft mount worked so well that we even shot at rabbits and deer across the canyon with deadly accuracy. The secret to the mount was to replace the recoil springs with tunable air-cylinders. High speed (1000 frames / sec) movies showed that there was very little or no recoil vibration.

Along with that I was the project engineer on a NATO twenty-five mm machine gun called the "Bushmaster," that we purchased from TRW. As fate would have it, Bill Smith, who had worked with Paul Stahlhuth and me on the Poseidon HPU was the responsible engineer at TRW on this weapon. Therefore, the technology transfer went very well. This NATO machine gun fired armor piercing, twenty-five mm-depleted uranium bullets or anti-personnel flechettes at two hundred–forty rounds per minute.

SS&V Program

Philco Ford had a thirty five million dollar contract with the Air Force called GAU7A. It was to build a gattling gun for use on the X-15 fighter aircraft that shot six thousand rounds per minute of caseless ammunition. The gun had six barrels rotating at one thousand rpm. What was unique about our gun was that it did not have the conventional chain-belt drive and heavy non- disposable brass cases. When our company was three months into the program, the Air Force discovered that we didn't have part of the contract in place and they informed our program manager that he had ninety days to come up with and to demonstrate a SS&V (Safety, Survivability and Vulnerability) Program for caseless ammunition or our contract would be cancelled. Being familiar with Air Force Contracts, and having had solid propellant experience at JPL and having had worked on a single shot, twenty-five mm, solid propellant cannon at Philco Ford, along with a twenty-five-mm machine-gun, all of a sudden I became the SS&V expert and found myself alone on an airplane headed for the Eglan Air Force Base in Florida with a four-volume contract to read and a few engineering drawings to review. I was told to meet with the Air Force General in charge of the contract and to get debriefed on what he expected of us to do.

Fear and trembling, sweat and a lot of prayer were my companions on the airplane that slowed my cramming down to zilch until; God sent his angels to calm me down and not to worry. Little did I know that professors from MIT, Cal Tech and The Armory in Maryland, who were the country's top experts on ordnance and aircraft weapons, would be at this two day technical conference with a live demonstration of General Electric Company's existing standard brass case, chain-belt driven, competitive gattling–gun and their SS&V Program. After spending my share of the two days on the hot seat at this awesome and intimidating conference, to say the least the Lord prevailed.

Intumescent Paint

For the next three weeks, I was assigned to accompany Air Force Capt Koester touring every armory, every solid propellant manufacturing company, every NASA test site in the United States and to visit the experimental F15 Fighter production line, with the highest US Air Force priority available. We were a two-man, ad-hoc committee assigned to find a solution to fire prevention for use of caseless, solid propellant ammunition on military aircraft, using the Philco Ford GAU7A weapon. On the last day of our tour our findings were pretty grim when our flight was detoured and we were dropped off at Moffett Field in Sunnyvale, California.

While we were waiting for an Air Force airplane to take us to Orange County, only by the Grace of God did we accidentally meet Dr. Sal Riccitello, who was heading up a fire prevention program on civilian aircraft at NASA Ames.

He introduced us to and demonstrated an intumescent paint that he was developing. This paint acted like the old-fashioned Fourth of July snake that would smolder and swell up to a hundred times its original thickness, forming a lightweight, closed-cell structure that would not burn and acted like an insulator. This was like manna from heaven and Dr. Riccitello was hired as a consultant to help us apply the technique to our ammunition system.

Within the allotted ninety days, Philco Ford built and demonstrated a fireproof, engineering prototype ammunition system and proposed an SS&V program that satisfied the Air Force requirements and saved our contract. Although, the Grace of God had prevailed on this project

Philco Ford eventually lost the program because we couldn't develop a material for the gun barrels that could last the full duration of the tactical mission.

X-ray Enhancement Machine

The train didn't stop after the SS&V program came to a halt. I got a call from the VP of Engineering asking me to take over and finish an Air Force fixed price fixed fee, contract at Wright Field, Ohio. Philco Ford had contracted to design and develop an automatic x-ray enhancing machine that would scan and measure the density of questionable areas of an existing x-ray and convert them into five-color images. The prototype had already been built and demonstrated but; the time and money were gone and the project engineer had quit. My job was to take over the defunct project and to make it work and deliver it to the Air Force Materials Lab as quickly as possible with least cost overruns.

When I said, *"the train hadn't stopped,"* it was a pun. What the engineer had done was to use an HO toy train as a conveyor and ran it in a totally dark circuit to process camera film. Cassettes of black and white, seventy mm photo film were first exposed under a densitometer and coded for density. The single frame film was loaded into stainless steel cassettes that were transported to three tanks of developing fluids and rinse water and were vertically raised up and down to agitate the solutions. After processing the film, the cassettes were hot air dried and released to a conveyor belt that brought the images to a tri-colored light projector that overlaid the three images onto a projection screen, which clearly showed non-uniform discontinuities and gradients in the material x-rayed.

Although, we won the battle we lost the war again. But all was not lost; on the way home, from Wright Field, the airplane stopped over in Kansas City, Missouri to pick up some passengers. A passenger who got on board sat next to me; he had just come from a funeral where he had to bury his very dear brother. This poor man was in sore need of comfort. During dinner before we got back to Orange County, Jesus came into his heart along the way home and he became a giant witness for the Lord thereafter, in the Fullerton area.

Fotomat

FOTOMAT came on the scene in 1968. Mary and I got carried away and bought a franchise in Fullerton, California. to supplement my engineering salary and her involvement with a modeling school in Newport Beach.

It was a cute little orange and yellow Kodak Kiosk in a popular parking lot near the Fullerton Jr. College. The mayor and the news media all came down and we had a very formal ribbon cutting ceremony and the whole nine yards. We even got to be king and queen for a day.

In as much as we were also involved with a college and career age singles group at our church in Orange, we had no problem getting good-looking college girls to work there. They were dressed in their cute little orange and yellow costumes and hats and Mary did their make-up and trained them in modeling. This all sounds like the kind of a winner that we all look for. The little island Kiosk did so well for awhile that we had three armed robberies at night and our girls quietly dropped out and business took a downward spiral.

The police force in Fullerton wasn't adequate to cover us as well as we needed. Undaunted, we didn't quit until within a year, Kodak sold their business to another firm that squeezed the profit out of our business and they bought back our franchise.

The singles ministry at the church continued to grow and Mary and I grew in grace along with it. Youth Pastor Dick Murray even baptized me one night in a swimming pool at the urging of the transitional Hippies. Can you imagine a fifty-year-old man who had by then been a Christian for twenty years, without being baptized and what a triumph that was for those young folks? What I learned from that is that God never gives up on you when he has chosen you to be one of his family. There was a big gap between the world's high places and what God had in mind for us when we volunteered, earlier to stand in the gap.

We might add, at this point in our family life, our own two beautiful teenaged, Christian kids were being taught by the schools to resist and question all authority and parents and especially churches. The Hippie generation was on a rampage and we lost control. What do you do? We had to choose between "us four and no more," or going forward with the ministry which God had called us out to do and that which we promised to do. Because we chose to follow the Lord and trust him to keep his promise concerning eternal salvation for our own kids, our lives have not been easy but God was able to share his manifold grace with us as we grew up daily.

An old hymn that we liked had words like, *"God works in mysterious ways, his wonders to perform, and he walks upon the waters and rides upon the storm."*

CHAPTER 12

Lasers
[1972-1998]

ILC Technology Inc

ILC Technology Inc was a high-tech lighting company founded in 1968 by Jack Moffat, a Cal Tech and Stanford Alumni friend of Allen Puder's. This company was in the business of making quartz bodied xenon and krypton arc lamps for electro optical devices such as lasers, lightships, aircraft safety lamps, landing field lighting approach glide path indicators, aircraft obstruction tower lights, space satellites and copying machines.

The first time that I looked at a flash lamp, I wondered why it took such high-powered engineers to build these simple looking little flash lamps. Jack Moffat educated me on the technology associated with the design and building of a quartz flash lamp and why it was called a high tech device. It turned out that the company logo (ILC) is an acronym for the basic design parameters of a flash lamps output quality; where; I = current, L = inductance and C = capacitance using various ionizing gases at various pressure levels to

237

achieve the proper wave length, duration and etc for the beam.

In September of 1972, I received this phone call from Los Altos, California. It was from my dear friend and old partner, Allen Puder. *"I am the equipment division manager of a company called ILC Inc in Sunnyvale and need your help. Can you come and be my operations manager?"* He further offered to let me stay in his guesthouse while I got settled down. Philco Ford was going through a recession and had just cut me back one salary grade from principal engineer to senior engineer and we no longer owned a Fotomat business, so I accepted but Mary didn't want to move which created a few new problems.

After two months of looking for a house big enough for our pool table, a grand piano and bible studies for singles, we finally found a match next door to Harry and Margaret Kallshian, the mayor of Los Altos. The house was fifteen years old and needed complete gutting and remodeling, which I did on weekends and late at night from November through February, when Mary, Nancy and I moved in. To compound our problems, it started to rain heavily from October until March and all of the streets were constantly flooded and it even snowed in Los Altos that winter. Mary and Nancy were very unhappy campers that winter. Nancy had to start high school in the second semester in Los Altos and Mary had to move into a house being remodeled and it rained every day for several months.

Peninsula Bible Church

One of the saving graces was that PBC (Peninsula Bible Church) in Palo Alto, CA had a young singles group starting up under Pastors Ron Ritchie, Ted Wise and Roy Thompson. They had about one hundred college and career-aged singles that were of the Beatnik-Hippie generations and met at a restaurant every Sunday. Having come from the same kind of ministry in Orange, California we thought that we could fit right in. But the leadership said that we didn't have the right credentials because we were too old at fifty and were married. We just hung around anyway and when the group got to be over five hundred and fifty and the fire department made us divide. We were invited to become part of the leadership and stuck with them for twenty-five years loving and caring for many scores of individuals, some of whom became Yuppies and Dinks.

Then Allen introduced me to the equipment division's charter to build the equipment, to not only manufacture the lamps but to also build the sophisticated electronic equipment to operate and performance-test each lamp. My job was to be the operations manager of the equipment division.

Dave Morman, electrical engineer and Jack Clove, designer were already working for Allen and became part of my staff. Jack Clove was the first designer that I hired when I worked at Borg Warner for Allen. Jack was without a doubt one of the most creative and the fastest designers that I ever knew and I was delighted to be working with him again. Dave Morman was part of LARTECH, which I had an interest in and was fortunate to work with him. He was a hands-on electrical engineer that went with the equipment to install and trouble shoot it in the field. Dave had served two years as a bush pilot missionary in Borneo and was married to a lovely lady from Australia, who had two of the very early USA designed stainless steel hip transplants.

Disc Laser Amplifiers

My very first job at ILC was to go to The Naval Research Lab in Washington DC to meet Dr. John Emmett a laser protégé scientist of Dr Arthur Schawlow, co-inventor and Nobel Prize winner for inventing the laser.

Dr. Emmett had built the first successful face pumped disc laser that used ILC flash lamps for pumping the laser. The problem was that our lamps were exploding and destroying thousands of dollars worth of equipment and very expensive neodymium doped laser glass. I had only heard about a laser and had practically no knowledge of how one worked so the first thing was for John to give me a quick short course on laser technology and how our flash lamps were involved. It turned out that this beautiful gold plated laser had an array of thirty-six flash lamps circumscribing the linearly arranged laser glass discs and used polarized dc electrical power from a capacitor bank charged to twenty thousand volts to flash the lamps.

As providence would have it, I had just finished working with an Atomic Energy Company in San Diego, California on a magnetic energy tube welding machine where they used the pinch effect created by running large pulsed dc currents through parallel conductors arrange circumferentially around two concentric tubes to be bonded together without the use of conventional welding or explosive bonding methods. When I was shown the construction of the laser, it seemed to me that this could be happening on the laser causing huge inward bending moments on our lamps.

With this information I proposed to try alternating the polarity on every other lamp to cancel out the magnetic affects. Jack Moffat and I worked with Dr Krechmer a physicist from SRI (Stanford Research Institute) to calculate the forces on the lamps and Jack designed the circuitry to pair the lamps. I built a crude test device for testing half of a lamp array that proved the theory. I worked with Jack Clove to design a clamshell laser cavity with soft mounts and built in crenulated reflectors. The laser glass discs were mounted on a precision stainless steel rail at Brewster's angle, such that each laser glass disc was independently removable. A full length cylindrical Pyrex-glass "shatter shield" was incorporated in the design to protect the laser glass as well as to provide a nitrogen filled acoustic chamber for deadening the shock waves created by the air ionizing in the laser cavity and discharging ozone. A new resilient lamp base design also came out of this project.

ILC was given a small contract to build a prototype test unit for the Naval Research Laboratory in Washington, DC, which was very successful. Subsequent to this success, Dr. Emmett was given the job of heading up the Lawrence Livermore Laser Lab (LLLL) and used ILC'S basic clam shell design for all of their laser disc amplifiers up until they exceeded the effective size of discs designs and switched to rectangular slab laser amplifiers. Drs. Orv Barr and John McMahon took over the laser laboratory at NRL with Bob Burns, technician. ILC built six production, seventy millimeter, clamshell type laser amplifiers for Orv Barr to perform research experiments in the plasma physics department at NRL. Orv and I still correspond regularly.

The Big Three

Fortunate for ILC, both Dr. Schawlow and Dr. Emmett were on ILC'S board of directors and Jack Moffat, president and CEO, worked together with them to develop xenon flash lamps of all sizes and energy levels for all of the generations of laser models built by LLL, including the present design of the NIF Laser, which will be the worlds largest glass laser when it will be completed in 2003 or 2004.

Unfortunate for ILC was that Jack Moffat was suddenly taken from us by a heart attack in 1986 and ILC was never the same. Jack and I and his family had become very close friends and I will not forget the times that we shared riding to work discussing work related issues and family problems as well. The only way that I can adequately describe Jack is that he was a prince of guy in all that he did or attempted to do, what a friend he was. *"To have a hamburger with Jack Moffat at Marie Callender's Restaurant was like eating with the king."*

A Car Pool

As a bit of humor, one Saturday afternoon in 1977, Dr Emmett stopped by ILC to visit Jack Moffat and me. He related this story that happened to him that week. It seems that he got a frantic phone call from his wife saying that he had to come home immediately. He dropped all serious laser business at LLL and raced home to discover that his five-year-old son had filled his convertible car full of water with the garden hose.

After draining out the water, taking the seat cushions out, jacking and blocking the car up, taking the four wheels off and spreading everything out in the garage to dry, he asked his son why he did it. Little John said, "For this energy crisis I was making you a **car pool**." That was hilarious, until he told us the rest of the story. At about two o'clock in the morning, the door bell persistently rang so he got up and there were two Livermore Policemen standing there with big flashlights pointing to his car and saying, *"Sir you have just been ripped off, someone has stolen your wheels and your seat cushions."* Our sides sure took a beating over that one.

Miracle Procedure

In 1974, when my world collapsed and I was diagnosed as having cancer of the stomach; it was through Jack Moffat, who quickly and quietly arranged with his friends at Stanford to get me the best gastroenterologist, Dr. Bart Lally and a neurosurgeon, Dr. Phillips, at El Camino

Hospital to perform a miracle procedure that removed my entire stomach, fifty-five lymph glands, my spleen, my appendix and later my gall bladder.

This procedure was one of God's miracles in that it was still experimental and only two other men had limited survival time. What they did was cut my stomach off at my esophagus and pylorus valve juncture at the duodenum. The pylorus valve was then sewn shut. They then cut my small intestine from my duodenum at the jejunum and took the small intestine and made a small pouch that connected to my esophagus, without any sphincters. The dangling jejunum was then sewn into the side of the small intestine, without a sphincter so that the bile and pancreatic enzymes could flow into the gastrointestinal tract.

The entire operation took five and a half hours and most people and my wife had given me up for dead. But, God in his inimitable ways had other things planned for me. Seven weeks later, in spite of the pneumonia, hepatitis and phlebitis that I got from the operation, I was back on the job learning how to cope with the new gastrointestinal system. Twenty-seven years later I'm still learning how to cope with the ever-changing system. I am asked many times, "how do you eat, what can you eat, and how often do you eat?" The answer is I eat the same as I ever did, I have the same hunger symptoms, I eat anything except a lot of animal fat, and salad vegetables. These all give me gas and don't digest very well. Quantity wise I eat large quantities three or four times a day. With that, I take pancreatic enzymes and diarrhea pills, which keep me regular.

The first ten years was rather difficult because there was a great deal of pain associated with stretching of the small intestines, adhesions tearing loose and from refluxing when I lay down, so I sat up. Through my two chiropractors Dr. Culver and Dr. Fields, they have gotten my spine straightened out. I now can lie flat on my back without any regurgitation or vomiting. This is quit amazing since I don't have any sphincters. But, what is more amazing is that it took a chiropractor to help my gastrointestinal system to behave. Refluxing three or four times and burning my lungs every night is not a pleasant scene.

Every year that I grow older, my system degenerates and doesn't produce the kind of energy that I need to put in a full day but that's normal and I go from day to day praising God that I'm still here with great hope for tomorrow.

Friends and Pals

During my convalescent days, Allen Puder and Jack Moffat would stop in at my house very often to encouraged me to get well, but the one guy that I cannot forget is Joe Caruso, my fishing pal came every day to have lunch with me just because he loved me. I think that this crude but gentle big Italian glassblower had as much influence on my getting well as any one. Joe took me fishing on the delta many times those days, even if it was just for a boat ride or to have our hibachi going to make teriyaki and to keep warm. What a friend he was and still is. Both Allen and Jack are gone now and nostalgic memories cloud my eyes when they come to mind.

Charley Mayo and Harry Smistik

Two other friends that were significant in my recovery were Charley Mayo and Harry Smistik. Charley has a home in Reno, Nevada and one in Santa Ana, California plus a cabin at Papa Fernando's on the Baja. Charley was very kind to me and took me fishing on his boat out of Newport Beach, California and at his cabin on the Baja where we got lots of sun and lots of fishing. One time we caught a four hundred and ten pound thrasher shark on a rod and reel that took three of us two and a half hours to land and drag into Newport Beach Harbor. One time we caught a two hundred and fifty pound yellow fin tuna and many albacore that Charley canned.

Charley and Harry and I went deer hunting in Utah every year for four years, which was really good therapy for my ailing body. Harry would take me to his second home in Sun City, Arizona every year to play golf and to watch the Super Bowl game. We then headed to Mexico to fish and hunt. We would pull his boat down to Hermocilla, Mexico and hunt for pigeons and doves and fish for huge large mouth bass. From there we would go to Mazalan and ferry across to the Baja and drive up to Charlie's cabin and fish for totuava, yellow tail tuna, groupers, barracuda, trigger fish, and sierra mackerel. Some times the wind would come up with hurricane force and tear the cabin to shreds, requiring a lot of repair work.

Harry was a special kind of a guy; he was a retired master sergeant from the Marine Corps, who had a scarred-up, mean-looking Cherokee Indian face and limped with a bum leg from a trucking accident. He talked rough and looked the part, but when he and I were in our sleeping bags at night, Harry was a sweet mellow man; we even talked about spiritual values and how the Lord was working in my life. Harry suddenly got Alzheimer's disease and scoliosis of the spine and it was a tearful event for Charlie and me to visit him for the last time and to help bury him two weeks later.

Punta Pescadero on the Sea of Cortez

Eight of us from ILC flew down to Punta Pescadero in three private aircraft. We caught so many Marlin, hammerhead sharks, yellow tail tuna, Dorado, and sail fish, that we got tired catching them. God was gracious to me to workout the details of those experiences and good times into my ever-improving life.

The Wash Machine

Allen Puder, my boss and I spent many long days exploring new product ideas and ways in which we could improve our production equipment. A guy by the name of Dan Laske came to us one day with the idea of building an automatic mask processor for the semi conductor industry. This machine was the size of a washing machine that completely developed and processed masks for making PC-Boards. A drying machine was also required to complete the system. Dan convinced us that the semi-conductor industry would beat a path to our doorstep so we tackled the job along with a crew of technicians that he brought with him including "Little Joe" Schimmelphenig and Danny Heitzman, whom became among my favorite technicians.

Along with the Mask Processor, we designed and built a drying machine that used "Freon 12" as a drying agent, which stripped water off of wet parts and flushed it down the sewer drain. That worked very well and speeded up the conventional hot-air drying process. At this time in history it was not a well-known fact that "Freon" was polluting our upper atmosphere and OSHA started a campaign to eliminate the use of Freon, even as a refrigerant and as a degreaser. This became a serious industrial problem and we were forced to abandon the product line, thus making our system less attractive to the PC-Board manufacturers. Danny and Little Joe were such good all around technicians that our department got into designing and making all-plastic, chemical processing machines, associated with the lamp manufacturing, semi-conductor, and plating industries. These systems were very large and required more space than we had available, so we bought out one of our suppliers and started another department.

Danny also took over the soft solder seal making process for our flash lamps and a special department was formed to include Pam Frenzel, who later took over the department.

UVEX

Allen and I, in the meantime were working on UV (Ultra Violet Light) processing of various product lines. The most promising product was a UV ink-curing machine, which eventually grew into Allen founding a new company called "UVEX." It was a sad day for many of us when we had to go to his funeral. Late one night as he was closing up shop a vandal lay waiting for him and hit him over the head with a fire-extinguisher bottle and proceeded to spray him with the bromide chemical. Allen survived the incident and continued to work for several months, but succumbed to the affects of the chemicals and a concussion. He was as fine a man as I have known and his Christian walk was always an inspiration to me over the forty years that our paths crossed or went together. Brent Puder, his son who was like a spiritual son to me, got his degree in Chemistry and became an expert in making and processing UV Ink. He now runs the company.

Puder's Cat

Before joining ILC as Equipment Division Manager, the Puder family, including their Siamese cat was on their way to Massachusetts for Allen to join the Perkin Elmer Electro Optical Division, and they had to go by the way of Kansas City. When they got to Kansas City, one of the teenaged twin daughters discovered that the cat was missing. Janice appealed to the Kansas City News Paper to help her find her kitty. The news broke nationwide and every news media west of the Mississippi River carried the story. Three months later the kitty had found its way back home to Pasadena, California and it was taken care of by the neighbors. The amazing story made headlines again and the kitty lived to be over twenty years of age in Los Altos, California, where the Puders later moved to join ILC Inc.

Large Laser Systems

Dr. Leonard (Len) Reed, VP and Chief Engineer of ILC, became my boss after Jack Moffat passed away and Allen Puder left the company. Dr. Reed is a specialist in ceramic to metal joining and electron tube and vacuum technology. He and John Richter had a company, which they sold to ILC in 1971 and brought their expertise to the company. Dr Reed was in close touch with The Rutherford Laboratories in England and also with the LLL lasers.

While I was convalescing from cancer, he hired Paul Lavoi, who was working on his PHD in Laser Physics. Paul occupied my office and we later became good friends and colleagues building a laser system for the Rutherford Laboratories in England. I was in charge of the design and manufacturing of the equipment and for shipping it to England. We went to school at LLL Laboratory to learn what Dr. Emmett was doing at Livermore and we built a total system at ILC with class 100 clean room and all of the operational functions including the high energy, high voltage capacitor banks and electron switches. This system was very successful and Dr. Lavoi became well known in England. He was also training personnel from the University of Japan on large laser technology and use of ILC built hardware.

AWRE

In parallel with Dr. Lavoi's work, the Atomic Weapons Research Establishment (AWRE) in Aldermaston, England wanted to buy a large laser system from LLL. Since International rules blocked governments from selling technology to other governments, AWRE had to invite American Industry to transfer LLL's large laser system technology to them. ILC was invited to participate; therefore, Dr. Reed assigned me the job of bidding on the job with Irv Kovalic, sales manager of ILC. He also sent me to Michigan to interview Dr. Brian Guscott, large laser physicist to participate in the preparation of the proposal with the intent of hiring on as the Large Laser Department Manager if we succeeded in getting the job.

We hired Helen Gourley, a precocious optical specialist and technical writer to be our Proposal Manager. After three months of hard work and pencil sharpening we produced a fixed price, fixed fee proposal to deliver all hardware, drawings, process instructions, installation instructions, operational instructions and technical descriptions of all components for a laser system completely installed and qualification tested, within eighteen months. Both parties were subject to penalty clauses for missed schedules.

Two full weeks of negotiations in England resulted in ILC winning the job over The General Electric Company, our closest competitor. This was a plump contract for ILC in the amount of three point two million American dollars, one-half of which was paid up-front.

Hank Baumgartner

Henry Baumgartner, better known as "Hank" was one of the founders of ILC along with Jack Moffat, and Joe Caruso. He was vice president of finances (CFO) and it was my great pleasure to negotiate the AWRE contract with him. Henry, as I always chose to address him rather than Hank, and I worked around the clock every night, for two weeks at a beautiful Inn called "The Springs," near Tadley. We then worked all day at AWRE. Henry is a graduate MBA from Stanford and a wizard with figures. His large stature, booming voice and golden tongue commands attention, even with the Queen of England. My job was to explain every technical detail of the proposal to him and to review all of my three suitcases of costing figures. To be involved in the mechanics of dealing with the British Government officials, who got their blessings from the queen was no small fairytale experience for me.

During the day at AWRE we sat at a very large conference room table where thirteen physicists from LLL and ILC and a matching number from AWRE representing each component were questioned by John McCormick, chief negotiator from England and Fred West, Program Manager for the Laser. About ten engineering and manufacturing specialists were also represented. Dr. John Emmett from LLL was very prominent at the meetings because it was two arms of his Shiva Laser that we were going to build for AWRE.

Winning the contract was no small pickings for ILC Inc as it was the largest thing that ever happened at our company and with the up-front cash, Henry and Jack Moffat were able to build a brand new building for ILC to accommodate the laser and to build a new lamp factory for Jack and Joe. Jack hired an architect to layout the building with inputs from Dr. Guscott, the new Large Laser Division Manager, Helen Gourley, Chief Optical Scientist, Dr. Reed, VP of Engineering, Glen Sorenson, President and myself, Large Laser operations manager. Land was purchased and Jack completed the job on time and within budget so that the laser program could proceed on schedule.

The Helen Laser

Shiva Laser, named after the Greek Goddess Shiva was a ten arm laser designed and built by Dr Emmett's staff at LLL. It was an awesome work of genius that occupied a brand new four-story, class 10,000 cleanliness level, laser building over 100 meters long and 20 meters wide. The AWRE laser was a two arm Shiva Type Laser, named "Helen," and was the third largest glass laser in the world at that historical period. Last reports are that it is still functional and producing scientific research data. My clamshell amplifiers and high voltage, high-energy electrical connector designs are still in use on Helen.

Dr. Brian Guscott

In fulfillment of our contract with Dr. Guscott, or Brian to most, he came on board at ILC immediately after we won the AWRE contract, as Large Laser Division Manager. Hard work began without fanfare. Brian came to live in our house in Los Altos for several months while he got settled down and bought a house nearby.

He was an English born and educated physicist so it made our multiple planning trips to England with AWRE personnel much easier. We also met with his mother, Ivy who lived near Stonehenge and Salisbury. As the program progressed, Brian got married and Ivy came to live with them in Los altos, California.

Brian and I spent many precious days visiting English factories and suppliers so that we could buy England as much as possible. It was a great education for me just learning things like "Odds and sods, the loo, the cod piece, high tea and low tea, everything was bloody and that "H's" don't exist." I also learned not to say fanny around women.

My favorite quote from Brian while we were exploring England and interviewing various industrial sites was *"Let's agree to* ***just do it*** *and* ***apologize later."***

Penalties Pay Off

As the program progressed and as Jack got our new facility and offices built, we hired an additional twenty people to round out our department to twenty-six people from PhD's to flunkies on the pay roll.

As time elapsed and our side of the pond was moving smoothly it became quite apparent to Fred West, Program manager from AWRE that they were falling behind and would end up with astronomical penalties. We negotiated a deal with him to send us Bill Macconnell to work with us coordinating some of the logistics of the program. In exchange I would go to England and help AWRE prepare the laser building, which was being built by a civilian contractor who was heavily tied up in bureaucratic red tape. It was conjectured that I would be able to work around it by being his stand in. AWRE had an old WWI and WWII facility that was skimping by with make-do government budgets and trying to convert a sow's ear into a silk purse. The old two story concrete and tin shack had to be completely gutted and brought up to class 10,000-particle cleanness. It would have been much faster, cheaper and ten times better if they just started over but rules are rules.

God Moves in Mysterious Ways

I think that the lord had something to do with my going to England because when I arrived on site, the contractor met me and said, *"I was told that you were really tough, so my wife and I decided to go to a very remote lake in the North of England to prepare for your coming."* I said *"Oh, that's good." So he proceeded to tell me that while he was relaxing by the lake a young American couple came strolling by and stopped to say hello. They were on their honeymoon and it turned out that they came from Sunnyvale, California, which set off some bells. He said that he told them that the reason he was there was to get some relaxation before meeting a tough laser man from Sunnyvale. "So you see I have already met you. The lady was your nurse during your cancer surgery and you were their guru at some church and counseled them on marriage. Small world, and you have a pretty big boss." Wow! What a beginning and yet another day my wife and I were crossing the street in a strange town on the Thames and a car pulled over and yelled Hi George! Meet me in the pub next door." I never saw him before and he wanted to thank me for being in WWII. Awesome!*

Billeting

Henry and I did a little forward work and with Fred's help we got the first group, government housing in Tadley for two months while our solicitor (real estate agent) found housing throughout the Basingstoke and Tadley areas for the forthcoming crews. We had to also go shopping to buy bedding and towels for six families, which Dr. Guscott would be bringing for one year. In the mean time Henry and I lived in a youth hostel that was very sparse and cold, but we only paid seven pounds a day for the two of us.

While Henry, Mary and I lived at "The Romans Inn," my wife and I found a small three-room house in a little town called Mortimer and lived there from September through December. This little town of about ten thousand people was where Queen Juliana of Denmark took refuge during WWII. We lived next door to a bakery, which we loved and the town was so beautiful during the best fall weather that they had in a decade. The town was a typical storybook kind of a place where everyone shopped at the little markets every day for food, bread and coal.

Being invaded by fleas reminded me of my experience in France. We had to fumigate the house with flea bombs to get rid of them and had to suffer the embarrassment of public scratching. It makes me itch just to write about the fleas. One great thing that we learned, when our furnace wouldn't start and it was fifteen degrees Celsius outside, was to warm up the bed with a hair drier, which did wonders for the body and soul. This little trick still works when the house is cold and your teeth have a hard time staying together.

Our evenings were spent going to the live theatre that held about one hundred people. We were richly blessed and entertained by the wonderful English actors. One play that we really enjoyed was "The Diary of Anne Frank." It was so good that when we took a Euro-rail tour of Europe, we went to Amsterdam to visit where it all took place and we were awed by the historical scene along the canals. It was an eerie feeling walking up the stairs to the room and touching the walls and doors.

New Life in Jesus

Of significance was the encounter that we had with a young Christian family down the street from us in Mortimer, England. They had a huge red and yellow banner in their yard that shouted out, *"New Life in Jesus."* Since they were out in the yard washing their car and their little toddlers were playing there, we stopped in to say hello and their response was, *"Oh No! Don't come near us!"* Startled we didn't know what to say. They laughingly said, *"We have chicken pox." Oh!"* We said and backed off.

This couple said, *"Come and help us work at a little Methodist church in Tadley that we are helping to revive."*

The congregation consisted of six older women, five older men and two young couples with two kids. The church building was too large to heat up for that small group so they met in a small back room that had a full wall of glass overlooking a cow pasture. The Vicar only came every fourth week because his parish had four churches to cover. That didn't matter because one of the older men taught from the Bible and the small group sang all of the verses of two of Charles Wesley's hymns, a cappella, every Sunday and they sounded like a full choir. By the time we left England, the Church and Sunday school was growing and they became our very dear friends. They treated us and educated us on the celebration of Guy Faulk's Day and we reciprocated by finding a turkey and having a real American Thanksgiving Day including Brian's mother, Ivy and aunt.

Campus Crusade for Christ

To further enhance our stay in England, our good friend Lee Carlson from Turlock, California was living in Reading, England, about six kilometers from Mortimer. He was head of European Campus Crusade for Christ Ministries and also wanted us to help, so we helped. Lee had just gotten married to Maria, a BBC gospel singer and they were struggling along living in a very small cold, bedsit apartment. Henry, graciously reached out to the newly weds and shared a weekend at the Springs.

Lee used to drive me to London on Sunday night to attend John Stott's church, just off of Trafalgar Square in London, where several hundred career aged singles met even on nights undaunted by the rain coming down in torrents.

To see England spiritually alive and well was a highlight of our stay there. On a train ride that we took to Edinborough, Scotland we met an older man who was the custodian for the remains of Winchester Castle at Winchester Hall and who was a Gideon. He shared his testimony and the gospel with us and continued to correspond for many years until he passed on. What a delightful and encouraging man to have gotten to know. One time he gave us a tour of the castle and showed us King Arthur's legendary round table where Sir Galahad and his knights sat around.

San Martino Alla Palma

With Lee's urging, at the end of our stay in England, Mary and I, headed off to Macedonia, Greece to spend Christmas with five Campus Crusade Missionary girls living in Thessonaloniki. It was their first Christmas away from their homes in America and they needed encouragement. Although we didn't know them, we agreed to go. God had other plans and he sent us fifteen hundred miles north to Florence, Italy instead, to be with my WWII friends, the Borgioli's, at San Martino Alla Palma, whom we still visit and correspond.

What transpired was that we traveled all the way down to the town of Brindisi, on the south east side of Italy and upon arrival we were supposed to take the ferry to Greece. The ferry crew went on strike and we couldn't get a passage from Brindisi to Greece so we had to turn around and go back north to Florence.

Later on, three of the CCC girls in Greece became like daughters to us and have kept a continuing relationship. Debbie Ellis is still there and in charge of intensive care nursing in the hospital.

The Lord Giveth and the Lord Taketh

Sadness comes into every life and within a year Maria Carlson came down with cancer and went to be with the Lord so, Lee returned to the states to move forward. He re-married a co-worker and they raised two children, while he went to Trinity College and Seminary in Deerfield, Illinois and received his doctor of divinity degree. We have since lost track of Lee and his family.

My Clock Stops Running

By the end of November 1978, I finished my job of helping the English Contractor finish his job and my crew had all of the operational systems in place for Brian to pick up the baton and to complete the job of installing, aligning and qualifying the Helen Laser. Queen Elizabeth II publicly pushed the button to fire the laser for the first time in 1980.

Mary and I took the month of December to tour and vacation in Europe via Euro-Rail Pass that took us to Italy, France, Germany, Holland and Spain, which we earned and enjoyed. The details of that trip would cover a complete book by itself and is not covered here. *Miracle upon miracle was revealed to us as we followed the Lord through Europe.*

When we arrived back home, Bill Macconnell and I completed making spare laser components and shipped them to Brian. Then one day, just after my birthday in 1979, I went into work and collapsed at my desk. I collapsed and my clock stopped. The doctor said that I had to quit working or I would die, so that's what I did.

When I quit my job rather than being put on medical leave our income went to zero. The long hard road back to health had both good and bad days and our hope in the Lord never waned. Fortunately, we were able to cash in my small original stock option that had grown by a factor of four and our investment gave us an income and Sumi's makeup business in Los Altos was doing well enough for me to retire and to restore my health.

Bill Mac was hired full time at ILC in charge of manufacturing and facilities. He has long since retired to Bullhead City, Arizona and we stay in touch at Christmas. He and his wife Pam have left their share of memorable footprints in our lives. One crater that I left in their lives was when we went to London to visit the House of Parliament, which was in session. There was a big sign on the steps at the entry that clearly said, "**No Photos.**" In my inimitable way, I didn't observe the sign and when the Bobbie shouted out at me to, "**Stop,**" everything in Parliament stopped except me. Graciously, Pam took the rap for me. Dumb Americans!

Photography

Ever since I was a young man, I was interested in photography and had taken many WWII photos so I decided to enroll in a professional photography course at Foothill College in Los Altos. I soon learned from fifteen thousand dollars later that I had built a professional dark room in my home equipped it with the best enlarger and processing equipment available and mounting equipment. I also bought two medium format cameras and two thirty-five mm cameras with every lens.

Through my ex-secretary, Nel Alkamade, I became good friends with her husband Franz. He was a native born Dutch machinist working for the University of Stanford and was also the best amateur photographer in the Central California Coastal Camera Club Committee of Santa Clara, called the 6-Cs. He had his own dark room and print mounting room. By my joining the Santa Clara Camera Club, which was made up of mostly professional/amateurs, Franz became my practical mentor and we traveled all over America and Europe taking calendar quality photos.

My teacher Miriam at Foothill College in Los Altos was an assistant to Ansel Adams and had a very nice little cabin near The El Capitan. She was what was known as a wet belly photographer, and she taught me how to see beyond what my eyes viewed, by laying on my belly in the wet grass in Yosemite Valley with a macro lens. Her colored slide show creations and multi media presentations were the best in California at the time. Being a protégé of Ansel Adams, black and white photography was her specialty. Through Miriam's fine teaching and Franz's mentoring, I won both, the photographer of the year award at the 6-C's Club and at the Santa Clara Camera Club in 1981.

I learned that to be a real photographer one must not only take the photo, develop the film, print and enlarge the images and matte them for presentation as well. Slide photography is a category that does not require developing of your own film to retain the title of photographer. Slide photography can be very difficult because what you see is what you get and takes a good eye to capture a quality picture.

Miss Lorraine's Modeling School, in Los Altos needed professional photographs of men and women models so my wife, whose middle name is Sumi, started a make-up business called Sumi's. Along with my photography we both kept very busy making portfolios for the models.

Dark room hours to get one good photograph, worth showing in a show or in a portfolio, sometimes took all night and filled several large wastebaskets full of scrap prints from "8 x 10" to "16 x 20" in size. This turned out to be a very expensive hobby and started to wear me out instead of improving my health, so I decided to quit the business and sell my equipment to keep me from being tempted by perfection. The best things that came out of this whole venture was to see ordinary men and women being transformed into extraordinary beautiful missionaries and models.

To have produced an award winning black and white photograph describing God entitled, "The Alpha and the

Omega©, " that will be fully described in another book, was well worth every bit of the time and effort learning to be a photographer.

Consulting Years

After I had spent two years doing nothing but hunt and fish with my friends Harry Smistik and Charley Mayo, I regained most of my health and felt like going back to work.

Inta Inc. is a company founded by Drs. Leonard Reed and Paul Lovoi both ex-ILC Inc. employees. Their company was in the business of manufacturing ceramic to metal seals, gold plating, laser welding of aircraft jet engine parts and applied laser paint stripping of large military aircraft.

I was asked to come on board as a consulting project engineer for Inta's laser projects, which I did for two years. This was great fun for me because some of my former co-workers from ILC, like Helen Gourley and Mike Cresap, were also on my project team. In parallel with this account, my good friends, Henry Baumgartner, CEO of ILC Inc. and Joe Caruso, Flash Lamp Division Manager of ILC needed me to build some tooling and special projects for Lawrence Livermore's Laser Division's large flash lamps and to automate some flash lamp manufacturing processes at ILC. Everything went along fine until I became sixty-five and Uncle Sam decided that I was earning too much money to be drawing full Social Security benefits so I decided to hang it up and fully retire.

Retirement

My son Tom, who was between jobs in the computer world of corporate finance, talked me into taking up golf and also get a 286 computer to fill my spare time.

I don't know whether to kill him or kiss him because the simple game of chasing a golf ball around a five mile golf course can lead one down the path of a whole new life style of frustration, humility and stretching of one's Christianity to the limit. The devil had a field day with me and some of my most trying days with God was on the golf course. But, when I view the benefits of having taken up the game, I can only say thank you Lord for enlarging my path to include golf and for all of the footprints that went with it. I can't think of a golfer that I haven't liked or haven't been drawn closer to.

There is one golfer that stands out in my memories and that is Danny Heitsman, a co-worker, who died with a golf club in his hand and heart as we shared his last days. During the period when I was convalescing from cancer, my dear friend and colleague Danny Heitsman was struck down with cancer, as well; we spent some painful but rewarding days fellowshipping and praying together before the Lord took him home.

Computers

What the outdoor game of golf didn't razzle dazzle me with; the PC computer did. At first it was fun playing games like Pac Man and Solitary but then I had to learn a whole new language and life style in a strange and frustrating world of DOS, floppy discs, hard discs, software, hardware, cd's, rams, bytes, bits, megabytes, gigibytes, web sites, e-mails, scroll, escape, num lock, page up, page down, home, megahertz, dvd's, control-alt, mouse, cursor, flat screens, enter, menus, hit start to stop, links, dot net, and dot com, which I'm still trying to keep up and to cope with. Guess whose winning? My garage and storage cabinets that are full of obsolete stuff are way ahead. Heaven can't possibly be messed up like this.

Back to the Drawing Board

O n my birthday in 1992 the phone rang and a big booming voice said, "Happy Birthday you are seventy years
old get back to work." In another weak moment Henry won
again. This time he wanted me to take over Flashlamp
Engineering Management, which was full of worms. During
the next seven year period ILC Inc. went through a number
of company changes; we closed down our Yuma annex; we
beefed up our English operation at Q-Arc Inc. and John
Littlechild became the chief lamp engineer for both Q-Arc
and ILC Flashlamp factories; ILC got a new President, Dick
Capra and I became ILC's corporate technical coordinator;
we acquired a new plant in Massachusetts called CPI
(Converter Power Supply Inc.) and Mike Cresap totally
remodeled the plant and I worked with quality assurance to
establish vendor test bases and help draft the quality
manual; we got certified; we acquired and upgraded a new
large metal halide stepper lamp factory in Sunnyvale; we
merged with a Japanese company called YUMEX, making
large metal halide stepper lamps and automated lamp fabri-
cating equipment under Mr. Y. Chigi, president; we
revamped and automated and remodeled our soft solder seal
lamp factory; we designed and built Large Laser lamps for
the NIF facility at LLL; ILC was purchased and sold several
times in the last year that I was there and lastly I helped to
upgrade and rearrange the Aerospace factory and operation.
*After twenty-six and a half intermittent years at ILC Inc., I
finally retired.*

My Favorite Quotations

1. *Gaps*
   a. *"I looked for a man to make up the hedge and to stand in the gap before me...but found none." Ez. 22: 30 KJV (Oxford University Press)*
   b. *"George, you don't need to know everything about a subject, you only need to find the gaps and try to understand them." Dr. Arthur Schawlow, Physicist and Nobel Prize Winner. 1989*
   c. *"Our job is to fill the gaps" Pastor Bill Jenkins 2000*
2. *4-Ups by George Oiye 2001*
   a. *"Just show up."*
   b. *"Listen up, to what is God saying?"*
   c. *"Shut up, so you can hear."*
   d. *"Look up, so that you can see."*
3. *"Sin doesn't just happen, we plan to sin." Pastor Ron Ritchie 1973*
4. *"We don't have the power to do, we only have the power to choose and what we choose determines*

what we do." Pastor Ron Ritchie 1973

5. *"Riding in a Rolls Royce in Washington is the perception of power and not the power itself that gives one power." William J Cooley, Lawyer and lobbyist 1976*

6. *"Why worry about the bust George, you didn't make it in the boom." Harry Smistik 1987*

7. *"Salvation is more than just a lifeline, it is also the anchor line." George 1979*

8. *"Salvation is more than just strings to pull with God, it is a lifeline." George 1979*

9. *"Look beyond yourself, George." The Holy Spirit. 1979*

10. *"Courage makes character visible." Pastor Bill Jenkins 2001*

11. *"God does not reward us for our scholarship, He awards us for our obedience to our scholarship." George 1975*

12. *"The Lord commends our faithfulness not our ability." C.I. Scofield, D.D. 1967*

13. *"We get educated beyond our obedience." Pastor Dave Roper 1973*

14. *"Sorry Comforters are you all. Is there no limit to your windy words?" Job 16:2-3 NAS 1973*

15. *"How do you choose good leaders? You don't, you grow them." George Oiye 1975*

16. *"To be a good leader one must first become a good follower." George Oiye 1975*

17. *"God is not in the business of protecting the flesh, it's a bad investment." Pastor Ted Wise 1975*

18. *"Spiritual Armor is to be worn on the inside to protect us from the flesh, our enemy and not on the outside to protect the flesh." George Oiye 1975*

19. *"The best kinds of parents are transparents."*
    Pastor Arvid Carlson 1968
20. *"Your kids don't need all the things that you give*
    them they only need you." Mom 1962
21. *"Love is the most difficult to fake." Pastor Steve*
    Ziesler 1977
22. *"They'll not care how much we know until they*
    know how much we care." Pastor Bill Jenkins
    2000.
23. *"Paradigms must go to zero before a change can*
    take place." Mgmt. School 1996
24. *"All the ways of a man seem clean in his own*
    eyes; but God weighs the motives." Prov.16: 2
    NAS 1973
25. *"Let's just do it and apologize later." Dr. Brian*
    Guscott 1977
26. *"Commit your works unto the Lord and your*
    plans will be established. Prov. 16:3 NAS
27. *"We are the God's workmanship created in*
    Christ Jesus to do good works which God
    prepared in advance for us to do." Eph 2:10 NIV
    (Zondervan 1973)
28. *"God never created us to be rats, so get out of*
    the rat race." Pastor Ron Ritchie 1774
29. *"I don't mind being a servant but I don't like*
    being treated like one." John Meyers 1975
30. *"Living without God is sin." Pastor Ron Ritchie*
    1973
31. *"Study to show yourself approved of God, a*
    workman who need not be ashamed handling
    accurately the word of truth." 2 Tim 2:15 (NAS
    1973)
32. *"You are my witness and my servant.... whom I*
    have chosen," Is 43-10 (NAS 1973)
33. *"There are only two ways to live your life. One*

as though nothing in life is a miracle. The other is though everything is." Albert Einstein
34. *"Eventually all things come together and a River Runs Through it." Norman McClain*

Epilogue

This has been the most rewarding accomplishment that I have ever completed and am ever grateful for the encouragement, patience, and support that my wife, Mary Sumi, has given me for over fifty years of living in this book and to endure a writer's needs while writing. Thank You.

Mary Jane Moffat how do I thank you adequately for your friendship, love, encouragement and editorial comments?

Also, thanks to every one that has ever left a footprint in my life and *most especially to the Lord for the biggest ones when you carried me.*

I am looking forward to writing several other books and booklets to fill a few gaps left by this one.

The Villages

Six months prior to my final retirement from ILC my wife and I were fortunate to sell our house in Los Altos for a premium price and to buy a retirement home at the Villages Golf and Country Club in South East San Jose.

Much like fools gold; all that glitters is not gold. The opportunities and amenities for retirement here are ideal, but poor health and arthritis have no conscience. For the first two years, more time was spent in bed than on the golf course until late Y2001 when the Lord opened a door for me at a chiropractor whose office is just outside of our gate. After a year of treatments three times a week, I am almost free of pain and am able to walk, to eat without problems and I will hopefully, play golf again when the weather warms up. We have also found a great church home within ten minutes from our house and are busy there, doing what we like to do. The problems that we are dealing with are that Sumi, who is the Concert Master of the Peninsula POPs Orchestra in Palo Alto, requires a lot of long late night driving to cope with and the fact that our doctors and friends are there as well. As Paul Harvey might say, "It will be interesting to see *"the rest of the story."*